Paul Mpagi Sepuya

Contemporary Art Museum St. Louis

aperture

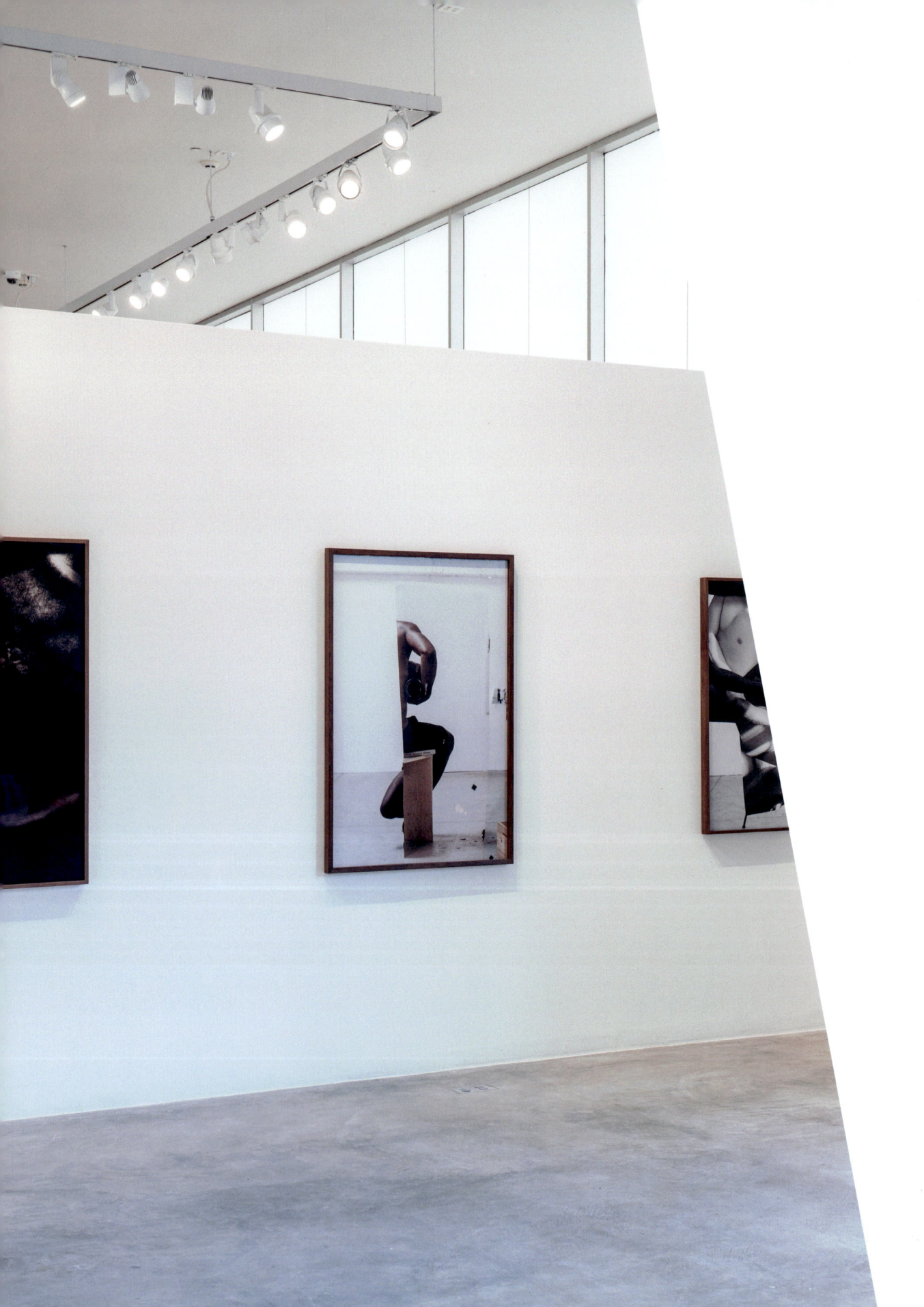

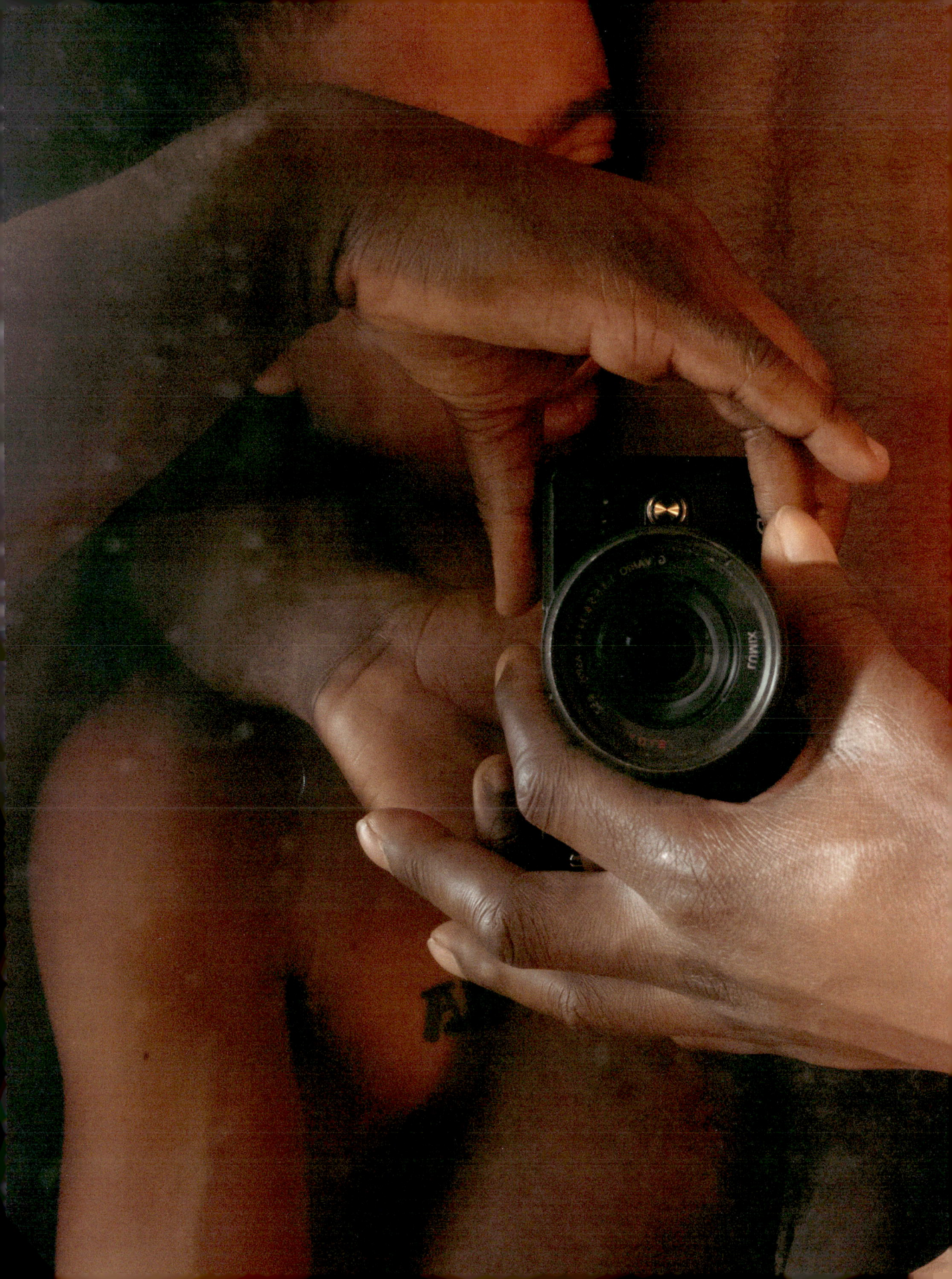

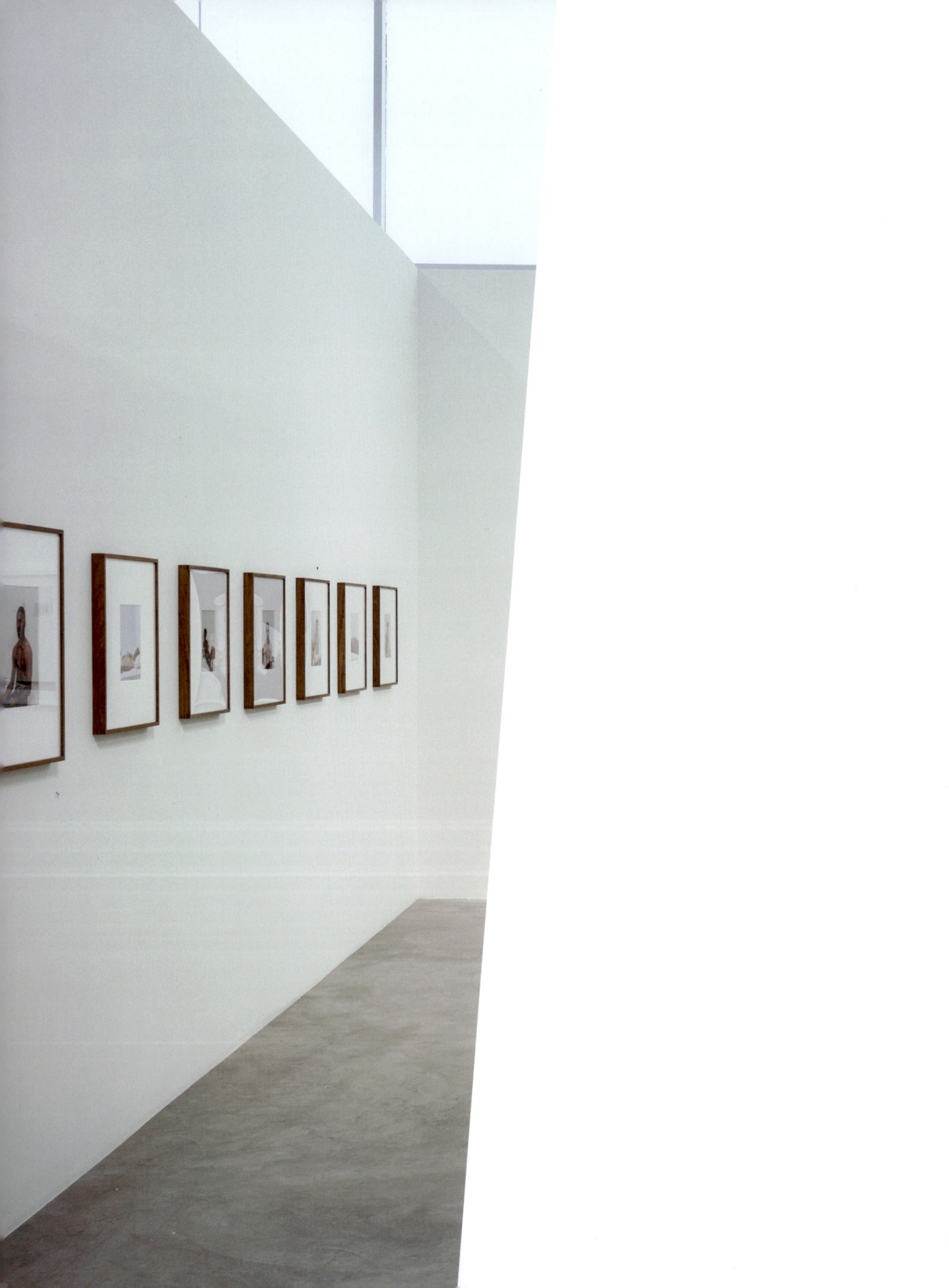

Contents

Foreword

The exhibition *Paul Mpagi Sepuya* is the first to survey more than a decade of the artist's practice. It offers the opportunity to trace visual, thematic, and conceptual connections across several bodies of work as well as to chart the artist's evolution in image-making. While we are privy to different strategies and varied nuances in his work, Sepuya consistently makes photographs that deconstruct traditional portraiture, challenging notions of "sitter" and "subject," and recasting the space, idea, and presence of the studio. His photographs feature friends, artists, collaborators, and himself, offering the perspective of a black, queer gaze. Figures are often rendered as abstractions through layering, fragmentation, mirror imagery, and shadow. Sometimes the body is represented only through traces left behind—of fingerprints, impressions in a velvet backdrop, fingertips holding a drape. The portraits are movingly honest, made with no digital intervention; what you see is what was there. Sepuya's photographs expose their own making with the apparatus of photography as an integral part of the picture—tripod, clamps, lenses, and the camera itself. The resulting work, covering multiple periods of Sepuya's career and life, reveals a profound intimacy between artist and sitters, reflecting a poignant generosity of spirit in its transparency.

My gratitude goes to Chief Curator Wassan Al-Khudhairi for deftly organizing this powerful and beautiful exhibition. Her expert curatorial selection knitted together several bodies of work to bring a generous and enlightening understanding of Sepuya's art to the public. My appreciation extends also to Assistant Curator Misa Jeffereis for her assistance on the exhibition. I am grateful to the institutional and private lenders to the exhibition who enriched the presentation by sharing their work. I am thrilled that the Blaffer Art Museum at the University of Houston is also presenting *Paul Mpagi Sepuya*, so that additional audiences can have the chance to experience this important exhibition.

This volume is Sepuya's first institutional monograph, which offers original scholarship and brings much-deserved recognition to the artist. The publication skillfully contextualizes Sepuya's work and marks his significance for our time with contributions by Al-Khudhairi; Malik Gaines, writer, performer, associate professor, and director of undergraduate studies at New York University's Tisch School of the Arts; Lucy Gallun, associate curator of the Department of Photography at The Museum of Modern Art, New York; Ariel Goldberg, novelist, poet, and essayist; Evan Moffitt, writer, critic, and associate editor of *frieze*; and Grace Wales Bonner, fashion designer. Lucia|Marquand has adroitly produced this book, published in association with Aperture.

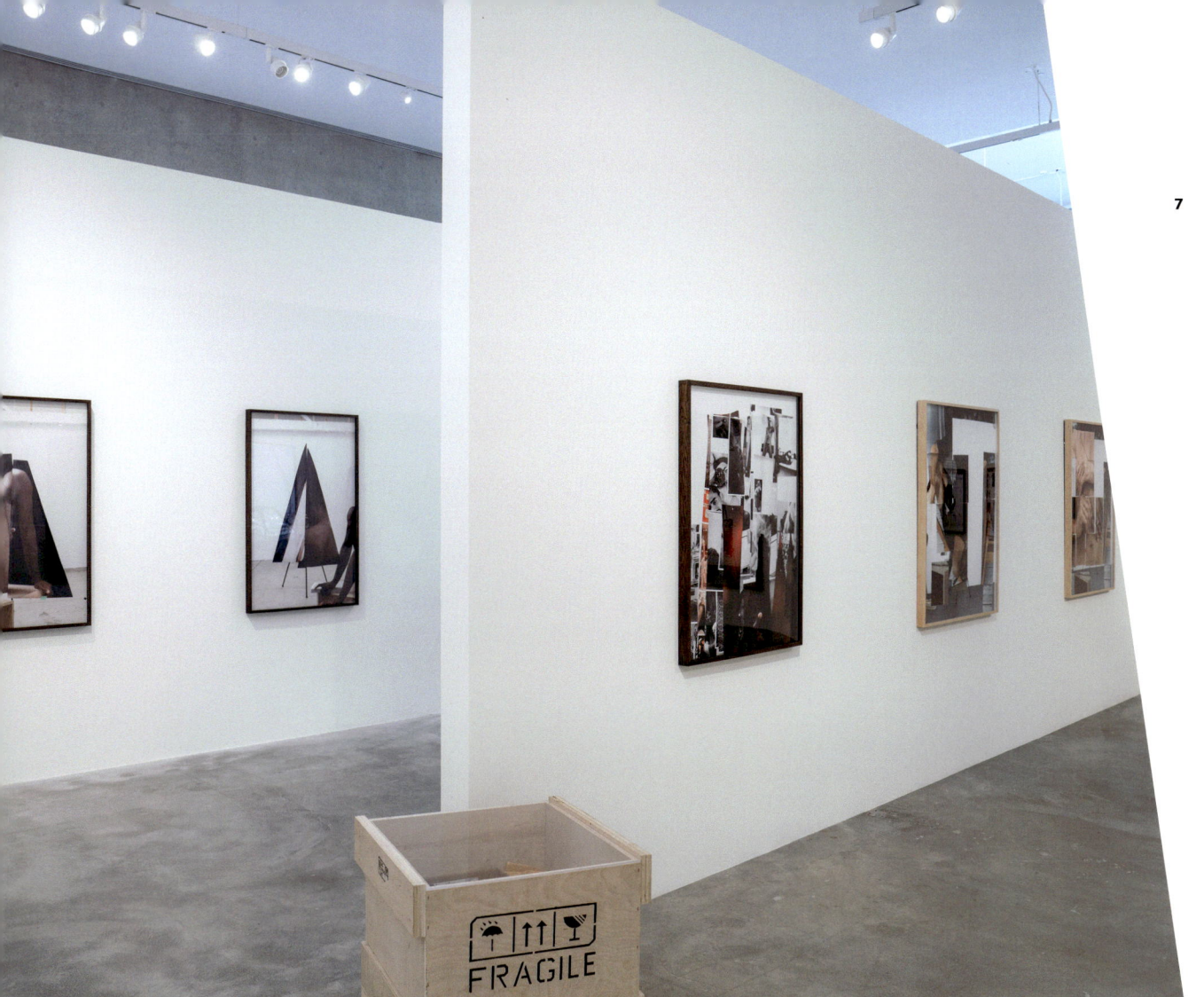

I add my own deeply felt gratitude to Al-Khudhairi's acknowledgments for the supporters of the exhibition and catalog: the Robert Mapplethorpe Foundation; DOCUMENT, Chicago; team (gallery, inc.); Vielmetter Los Angeles; Hedy Fischer and Randy Shull; Nancy and Fred Poses; Hunt R. Tackbary; Heiji and Brian Black; Thomas Lavin; and the Robert Lehman Foundation; with special thanks to Barrett Barrera Projects.

It was a great pleasure to work with Paul Mpagi Sepuya to bring this project to fruition. He is thoughtful, astute, and tirelessly committed to his work, adding a singular and potent voice to the contemporary art landscape. We are grateful to be able to share his vision through the exhibition and publication.

Lisa Melandri
Executive Director
Contemporary Art Museum St. Louis

Acknowledgments

I feel honored to have had the opportunity to work with Paul Mpagi Sepuya over the last two years to bring his exhibition and this publication to fruition. When I first spoke to Sepuya about organizing an exhibition of his work at CAM, I expressed my hopes for a presentation that would help audiences get a deeper look into his practice. This exhibition at CAM brings together works from over ten years and gives us the opportunity to trace the connections between bodies of work that are often otherwise difficult to see. The viewer can begin to enter into Sepuya's world—by seeing the reappearance of objects and people over time.

I extend my deepest gratitude to the lenders of this exhibition: thank you, Hedy Fischer and Randy Shull, Nancy and Fred Poses, Joshua Friedman, Mark McDonald and Dwayne Resnick, Sibylle Friche and Daniel Quiles, Columbus Museum of Art, Ohio, Lucy Baird, Cristina Vere Nicoll, and Lina Hargrett and Carlos Lago. Support for the exhibition and publication came from Hunt R. Tackbary, Heiji and Brian Black, Thomas Lavin, the Robert Lehman Foundation, and Barrett Barrera Projects. Without the unwavering and committed support from DOCUMENT, Chicago; team (gallery, inc.); and Vielmetter Los Angeles, this exhibition and publication would not have been possible. Thank you, Sibylle Friche, Aron Gent, Gabriella Caputo, José Freire, Susanne Vielmetter, and Ariel Pittman. After our CAM presentation, this exhibition traveled to the Blaffer Art Museum at the University of Houston: thank you, Tyler Blackwell, for reaching out and for working together to bring the exhibition to Houston.

My hope for this publication is that it not only offers the reader background on Sepuya's practice and examples of his work, but that it also captures his collaborative nature. I think we were able to achieve this thanks to the writers who agreed to contribute their work. I want to thank them all for allowing us to manifest Sepuya's spirit of collaboration here in these pages: thank you, Malik Gaines and Evan Moffitt, for writing about Sepuya's work from the perspective of a sitter in his studio; Lucy Gallun, for diving deep into one photograph and giving us a historical lens from which to view Sepuya's work; Ariel Goldberg, for helping us imagine what it's like to be alongside Sepuya to make photographs; and lastly Grace Wales Bonner, for capturing her impressions of Sepuya through the ongoing relationship of artistic exchange they have nurtured over the years.

Thanks to Adrian Lucia, for encouraging me and for always being excited about our projects. Tom Eykemans, I am grateful for your beautiful design of this publication, which captures the spirit of the artist's work and our CAM exhibition. Thank you, Lesley A. Martin, for being eager to collaborate with us to co-publish this book; we are thrilled to have this wonderful opportunity to work with you and your team at Aperture.

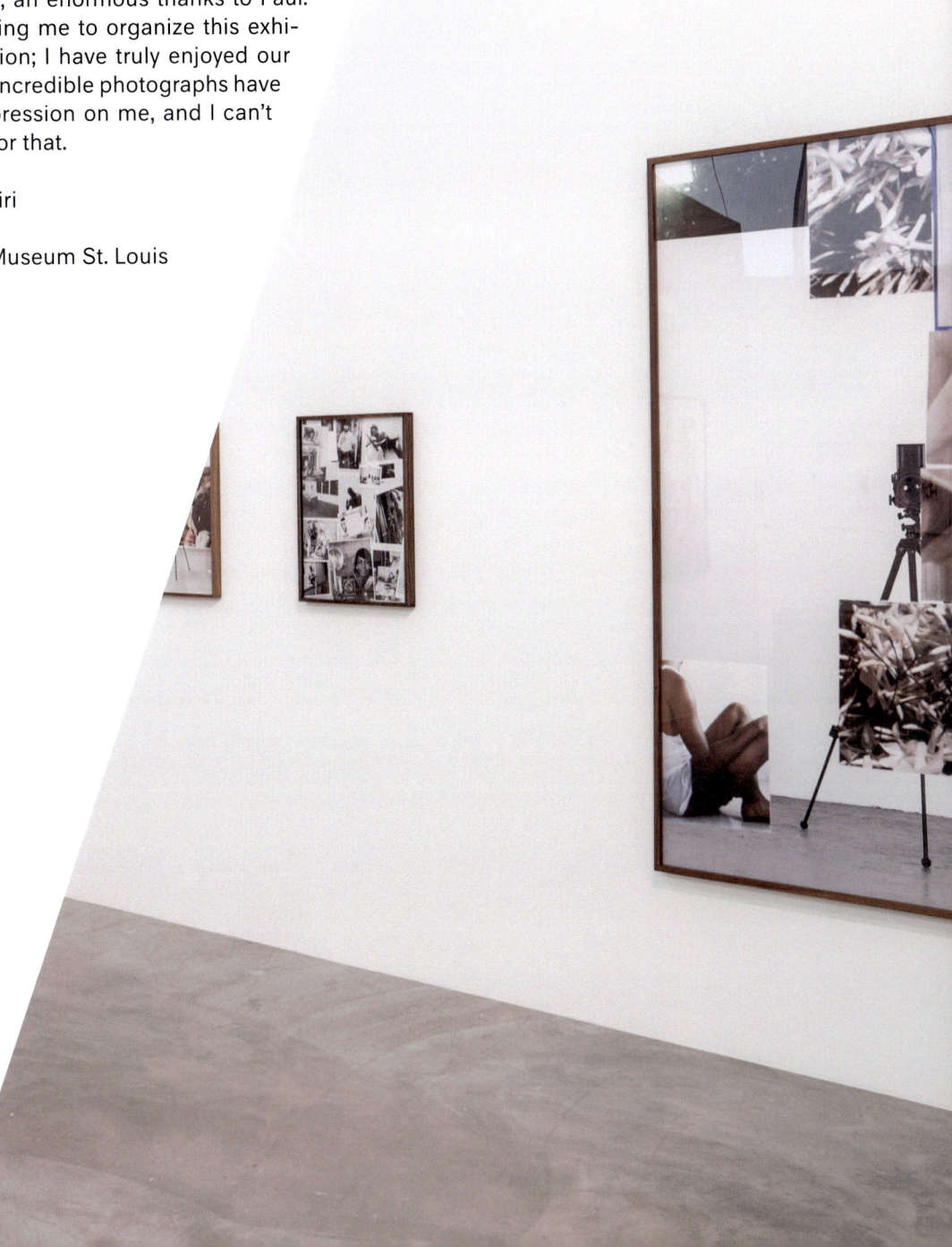

A huge thanks to the team at CAM, especially Registrar Jen Nugent, Assistant Curator Misa Jeffereis, and Communications Specialist Eddie Silva, for their commitment and all the hard work they put into this exhibition and publication. *Paul Mpagi Sepuya* is possible because of Executive Director Lisa Melandri's vision for CAM. She has created a museum that not only supports curators and artists but also is a space that allows us to think big. Thank you, Lisa, for your guidance and support.

And of course, an enormous thanks to Paul. Thank you for trusting me to organize this exhibition and publication; I have truly enjoyed our collaboration. Your incredible photographs have made a lasting impression on me, and I can't thank you enough for that.

Wassan Al-Khudhairi
Chief Curator
Contemporary Art Museum St. Louis

Interview with Paul Mpagi Sepuya
by Wassan Al-Khudhairi

WASSAN AL-KHUDHAIRI   Over the last two years, we have been working closely on your CAM exhibition. From the beginning, my intention was to bring together multiple bodies of work you've made over more than ten years, creating an opportunity to explore the progression of your work and the interconnectedness of your photographs. I've found that one of those interconnected threads is literature. Can you talk about the role of literature in your practice?

PAUL MPAGI SEPUYA   On initial glance, the work of writers may not be the first thing viewers think of when they see my work. But it has been that constant thread, as you mentioned, in my thinking about art making. My turn to literature developed as a way toward understanding portraiture while trying to make sense of my early projects. In the field of photography I couldn't find writing I was drawn to on the life and drives of the artist as valid material for critical thinking. But all of that was at the center of my work and what I was trying to understand for myself. I honestly wasn't drawn to sociology or cultural anthropology or visual studies more broadly. Literature, and specifically twentieth-century modernists' dealings with sexuality, offered a space where the text itself was the meeting ground of dynamic forces.

To talk about literature, I have to mention several of my projects that are not in this exhibition: *Beloved Object & Amorous Subject (Revisited)* [2005–06], which borrowed its title from Roland Barthes's *A Lover's Discourse: Fragments* [1978]; *Alexandria* [2009], based on Lawrence Durrell's *Alexandria Quartet* novels; and *Some Recent Pictures / a journal vol. 1* [2013], which is inspired by Richard Bruce Nugent and organized around a collision of narratives by Christopher Isherwood, Truman Capote, and Gore Vidal.

For many years I had been turning to the fiction, diaries, and other texts and images of British writer Virginia Woolf and Harlem Renaissance writer and illustrator Richard Bruce Nugent as guideposts to understanding portraiture. It is in Woolf's *Orlando* [1928] and Nugent's *Smoke, Lilies and Jade* [1926] that I began to see reflected my own drives to working in portraiture, the transformation of the author's and subject's instability into a text/image, and the author's desire and aim laid bare. I couldn't find a better text on portraiture, and so for a while I left behind writing on photography for these authors, along with Lawrence Durrell, Alice Walker, and others.

The first volume of *Some Recent Pictures* [2013] pulled a variety of seemingly disparate images and associations from my developing photo archive along with quotations and reproductions of texts and books by Isherwood, Vidal, and Capote. The photographs roughly trace many years of friendships and flirtations that developed around the making and dissemination of my 2005–07 zines. I was traveling a lot at the time and the prior zine work laid down a series of invitations that preceded my actual arrivals years later, so to speak. Capote's notorious 1948 self-portrait operated in a similar way. [For the jacket of Capote's *Other Voices, Other Rooms*, he posed recumbent on a couch, like a modern-day Oscar Wilde.] And I was thinking about genres and the author's aim as relating to the creation of a character (portrait) from a person (relationship) and how it was understood by the reader. In writings by Isherwood, Vidal, and Capote, there appears a thinly veiled biographical subject whom Isherwood calls "Paul," in a story of the same name, in his book *Down There on a Visit* [1962]. It was the convergence of these three authors through a single subject—whose real name was Denham Fouts, given the name "Paul" by Isherwood—that led to the beginning of *Some Recent Pictures.* It was through the process of editing that work that I made sense of my growing archive and photo journals, which continue to be a repository for source material in ongoing work like *Mirror Studies, Exposures*, etc.

WA Early in your career you made zines, and you have talked about zines as a tool to disseminate information. Is that how you came to making them, because you wanted to expand the dialogue around your photographs and to reach more people?

PS It grew out of a desire to share my work and to make my own opportunities. Zines were my way to initiate conversations with an audience in a format that was accessible and within my means. It was in those zines, and then increasingly in reproductions within other publications and online, where the work first developed an audience. I didn't anticipate what that dissemination would do to the work and our relationships to those pictures. By "our" relationships, I mean me and my friends as subjects, and the audience that became part of an expanding social circle and subjects themselves. The early work has had many lives.

By 2007 I was confronted with the effects of widespread dissemination of those portraits, on myself and on the other subjects, as well as our relationships to those pictures. I had to think about what it meant to be making portraits that circulated within the economy of homoerotic art and fanzine culture, such as publications like *BUTT* magazine. The photographs were made as art but developed a social currency on Friendster, Myspace, Facebook, and then within apps. Friends would tell me strangers approached them from having known the portraits. Several friends had fan art dedicated to them due to the images. A friend from New York moved on a whim to Buenos Aires, didn't know anyone there, and a couple introduced themselves at a café, asking him, "Are you Todd from Paul Sepuya's portraits?" These are commonplace occurrences, nothing special in the world of Instagram.

When I talk about Truman Capote as a touchstone, it's also because of Capote's understanding of how the currency of portraits could seduce and smooth the way for other kinds of creative and cultural encounters (not to mention erotic). As all of this was happening in 2008, for example, it was important for me to be able to recall Capote's 1948 self-styled portrait for his first book and the calculated game of exposure he was working.

WA In your exhibition at CAM there are a number of your early portraits. These photographs were made in your bedroom or the bedrooms of your sitters. Now all your photographs are made in your studio—and your studio is really the "site" of your photographs. Can you talk about the studio as site and how that evolved for you, from the bedroom in these early photos to the studio in later photos?

PS Yes, but first I want to mention that not *all* of my current photographs are made in the studio. The site of my Brooklyn bedroom happened as a logistical convenience and eventually became a subject of the work itself. I switched from working in the living room and kitchen of the townhouse I lived in with several friends, just so that I could be a better roommate—not leaving camera and lighting equipment in the common spaces, not having to clear out rooms and put them back together daily. But in moving to the bedroom, the intimate foundation of the project quickly came into focus. Those first tightly cropped bust portraits gave no hint of their location, and people spoke of them as if they were studio portraits. It was always important that I wasn't making work in an anonymous photo studio rental, that the intimacy in the photographs extended from the place of their making. So I began to pull back and reveal the horizons and landscapes of the bed, revealing the edges of bookshelves and other details. The bedroom became the recurring ground of the portraits. And by 2008, I had started photographing details of the room itself. I also wanted to get out of my comfort zone by making portraits in the homes of friends, which you see in several of the works in this exhibition.

The common threads between the bedroom and the studio are, first, they are continual, not constructed and deconstructed. Meaning they are dynamic and lived and worked in when not in "session." And second, they are sites that become subjects in and of themselves as the projects developed, through the repetition of being photographed over time.

WA What you have been successful in doing when transitioning from the bedroom to the studio is to keep that sense of intimacy and closeness—something that could have easily been lost. Is that something you were conscious of at the time?

PS Despite the change from home to studio, the intimacy remains, because I continued to work with the same (yet expanding) circle of friends; the images are extensions of friendships and relationships.

WA Who are the subjects in your photographs and what is your relationship to each?

PS The subjects in these early portraits were friends or acquaintances I was just getting to know, some of whom would become good friends, some with whom I would eventually lose touch. Some I have reconnected with. It was important in deciding to make portraits that they be of people with whom I desired friendship, platonic or romantic relationships. It was also a conscious decision that, regardless of the nature of our connection, the photographs would depict them as if they were, could be, or had been a lover. I wanted that kind of desire to be the foundation, to go all the way and then negotiate back.

The portraits preceding the selection in this exhibition became a project called *Beloved Object & Amorous Subject (Revisited)*, the title of which was quite a bold choice to borrow from Barthes when I was a twenty-four-year-old upstart. But it was that gap of language between desired object and desiring subject where the photographs sat—that was the spark for me.

So by the time I got to the portraits here on display, I had a body of work that had been produced and partially exhibited, and served as a foundation. These friends knew what they were getting into by then. And I was also playing with the desire of these subjects to be photographed, as they were aware their images would circulate in zines, artist publications, and online.

WA I remember one of our first studio visits, where you kept bringing out box after box of photographs for us to look through. There was a time when you were making a lot of photographs, and then something slightly shifted and you began rephotographing your own photographs. Can you talk about how this came to be—when and how did this shift take place?

PS Ah! Those boxes of old portraits. I love living with them, and once in a while, opening them up brings back so many memories. Those are all "straight" darkroom prints, and along the way I was keeping these private folders of snapshots of my workspace in the darkroom. Records of arrangements of test strips, outtakes, collisions of incidental material. But those were more akin to journals and nothing I considered artwork in itself.

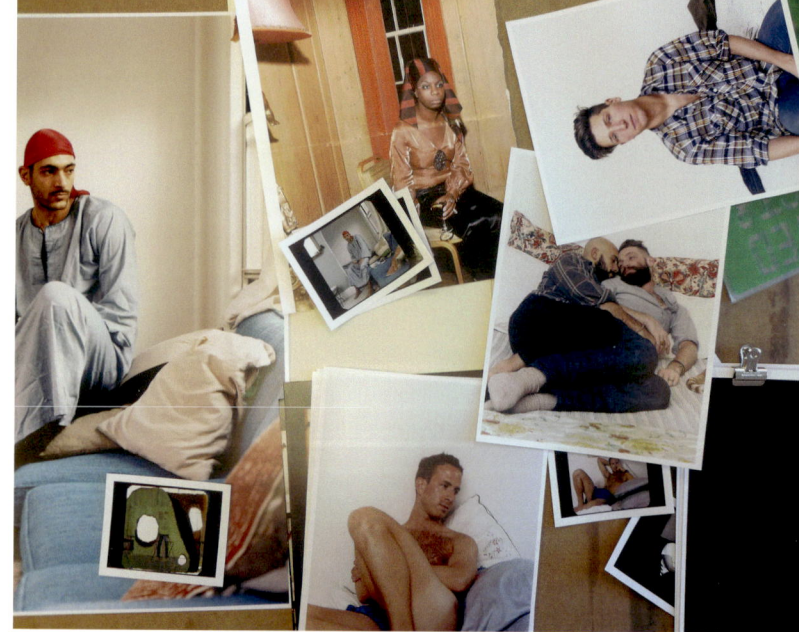

I had my first long-term residency at the Lower Manhattan Cultural Council [LMCC] in 2009–10. I used the residency like an office space, so I wasn't making photographs there. I had desks that I would use to lay out and organize prints that were made in a darkroom across town, printed from negatives shot at home. It was a place for presentation, and where I was learning how to display my work and have initial studio visits. And I continued to take snapshot "notes" as I sorted and organized material on those desks, akin to my earlier snapshots I printed in the color darkroom labs. Then I made a particular snapshot, later printed as a work called *Desktop, April 23rd* [2010, fig. 1]. It's just a photograph looking down at all of this mess on the tabletop. It includes fragments of several projects that I was working on simultaneously, all held together in suspension in that one picture: C-prints, Fuji instant film prints, test digital C-prints, a tear from a magazine . . .

After LMCC, I had a monthlong residency at the Center for Photography

Fig. 1
Paul Mpagi Sepuya
Desktop, April 23rd
2010
Digital C-print
Courtesy the artist

at Woodstock [New York], where I went with a plan to learn to scan negatives and learn digital printing. But I got up there and I had this space—an attic room around six-hundred square feet, maybe more. I thought to myself, "Oh, I have to use this space." I started a process using one of the digital cameras from the residency. It was my first serious attempt at using digital capture. I woke up early each morning, photographed myself and my surroundings, then biked down to the lab, edited, made large test prints, then brought the prints back to the attic studio, where I rephotographed myself and the material. This would accumulate and begin again the next day. And simultaneously I was receiving images from my friend Matija, who is a choreographer from Croatia. He was staying in my Brooklyn room while I was at Woodstock. He sent me pictures of himself in my home, and I incorporated those into the material I rephotographed, and that continued when he returned home and sent me photographs of himself in his flat in Pula, Croatia [figs. 2 and 3].

LMCC introduced the idea of a studio site that could hold disparate material in suspension. Woodstock introduced the process, recursive time passing in that space of the studio. Together they planted the seeds of what would become *STUDIO WORK*, a project of photographs and related personal archival material that came together during and immediately following my next residency at the Studio Museum in Harlem in 2010–11.

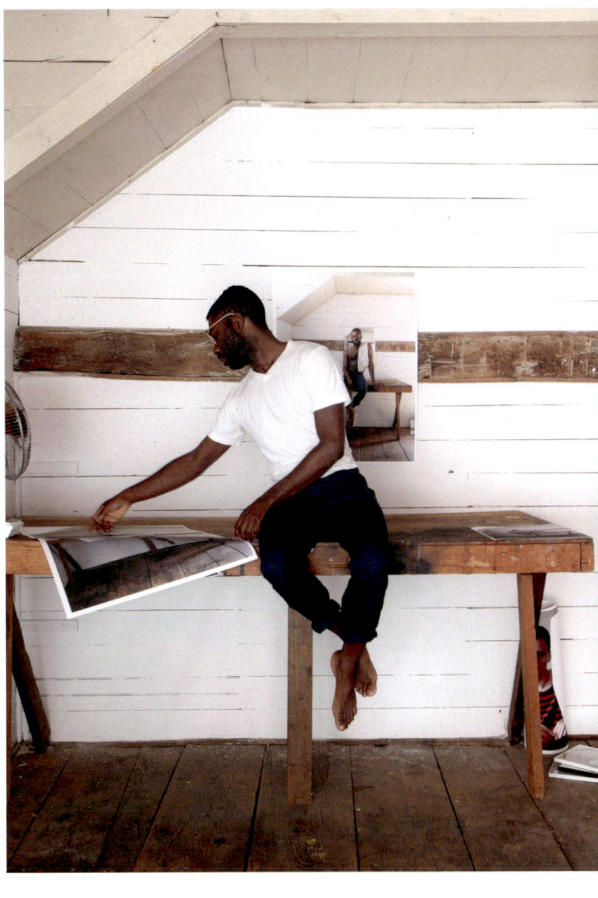

Fig. 2
Paul Mpagi Sepuya
Self-Portrait After (from the series *"Glasco Turnpike"*)
2010
Archival pigment print
Courtesy the artist

WA When you first started making photos you were using film, but you now make all your photographs digitally. Can you talk about what prompted this shift from film to digital?

PS As I mentioned before, at Woodstock I made my first considered photographs with the digital camera. Following that, during the Studio Museum residency, I got an adequate Lumix DSLR and switched to shooting mostly digitally. I was so comfortably and confidently precise with film and darkroom photography. It was a rocky transition, and I didn't know what I was doing. I shot on JPEG instead of RAW, if that gives you a clue.

It was about the speed and economy of cutting out the darkroom. So many photo labs were closing or getting more expensive, and I couldn't afford film anymore. Like at Woodstock, I wanted to be able to shoot, print out working material, look at it, keep the cycle going, etc. To make quick test material I would get ninety-nine-cent photo-lab prints and put them in dollar frames and keep them around the studio. *Darren, September 8* [2011, page 43] is a great example of the rephotography of these test prints in my studio. It features multiple images that appear elsewhere in the project in fragments or whole form. In its center is a test print of Darren from three months prior, behind which is a fragment of a portrait of my friend Joshua in a turban. And then there's also a little fragment of, I think, the books that I was reading that are actually on view in this version of *STUDIO WORK*. One of them is this book by Violet Trefusis, *Broderie Anglaise* [1935], and then there's also a little fragment of Woolf's *Orlando*. And there is a dried-out citrus peel, a recurring motif in the studio, and several succulents found their way into many of the photographs, subtly changing over time. I like how they introduced another cycle of linear time to the recursive loop of time in the studio . . .

But I'm digressing. Back to digital photography. The change was liberating for me because I was necessarily working outside of the studio between the end of the Studio Museum residency in the fall of 2011 until I moved to Los Angeles in 2014. I couldn't afford a studio but needed to keep working, so I bought an affordable laser printer, which I kept at home and used to quickly print what I shot. I had bundles of these laser printouts, bankers' boxes full. I would make smaller edits of a few dozen to a hundred or so printouts bound with binder clips, but they were largely unfinished and overall unresolved. The digital became analog material.

Shooting digitally was very freeing but also led to a crisis of shooting "too much" and, what I feared, could be a lack of focus. During this time I was able to travel quite a bit—some for work, some for my own projects. I was going between New York, LA, Paris, Barcelona, Berlin, and Denmark—connecting and collaborating on art with people that I had only had friendships with through correspondence, either since the zine days, or through things like *BUTT* magazine, or Friendster and Facebook. So a lot of this project is about being in all these places and photographing these people, with me being part of that project. The material became an overstuffed diary that needed transformation into memoir, autobiography, fiction, gossip . . . back to literature, you see . . .

WA Can you talk a little more about *STUDIO WORK*, because it's not a fixed work? What does this work mean to you and how did it come about?

PS So *STUDIO WORK* was bringing together that snapshot *Desktop, April 23rd* and the cumulative image-making strategy from Woodstock to the portrait-making process. I began inviting my friends, with whom I'd been making work at home or in their homes, up to my residency at the Studio Museum. To be honest, I began that residency not knowing what the project was or would become. However, I had a strategy and a starting point. I was also rereading Woolf, Bruce Nugent, and then particularly Brian O'Doherty's *Studio and Cube* [2007],

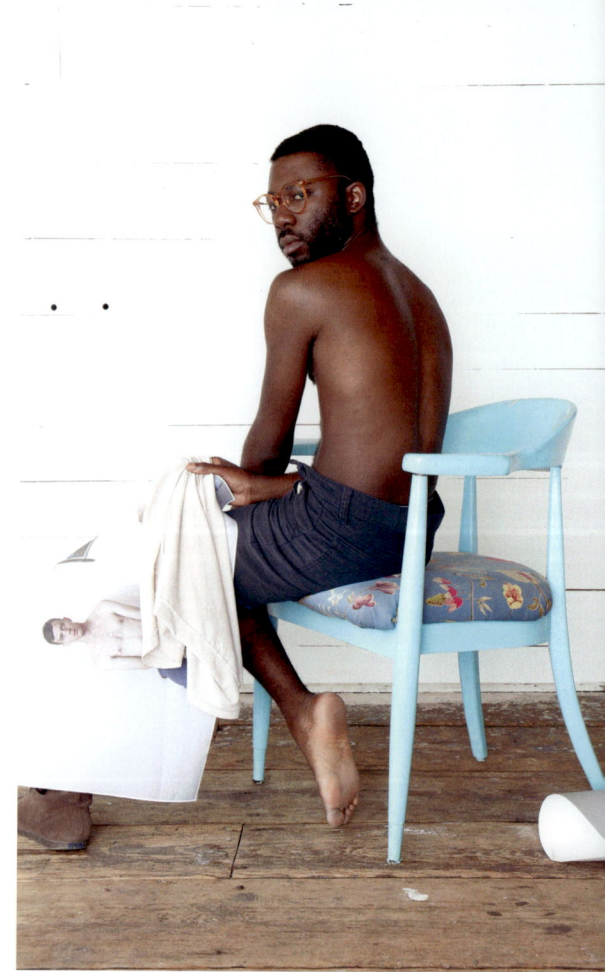

where he talks about "studio time" and something like the collage of compressed tenses that happens in the artist's studio. It was an "*aha*" moment, if an "*aha*" can unfold gradually.

The contents of *STUDIO WORK* are the work prints, outtakes, laser prints of portraits that I made during the residency. There are bundles of material I was editing. Books and articles that I was reading. Objects and content that friends brought and left behind in my space. *STUDIO WORK* is the archive, constantly open to reorganization, of photo and print material accumulated from beginning to end in the residency. From that source can be pulled discrete photographs, which have been produced in previous solo presentations of the project, that are hung on the perimeter of the gallery space while the tabletop and/or crate is installed at the center. Past exhibitions of *STUDIO WORK* have all been different—different materials pulled and displayed, others hidden, no two arrangements the same. Each is made on site. And because I continue to work with, have conversations with, and spend time with the subjects, I like that process of opening up the boxes and being continually influenced by those relationships, and by what is happening in my studio at the current moment. So when you come to this exhibition and see *STUDIO WORK* [pages 39–41], what you get is a partial excavation of a crate, presented both within that crate and in a tabletop vitrine.

WA How did you transition from printing, bundling, and pinning up your photographs to experimenting with mirrors?

PS I'd been thinking about wanting to get a mirror to photograph in for a while. When I moved back to Los Angeles in 2014, I went to visit my artist friend Matthew Savitsky [Minty], who lived in San Diego in this house that he shared with other UCSD grad students. They had these giant mirrors that Minty found on a construction site or someplace, and I took several snapshots of them and kept printouts in my new studio at UCLA. They made their way into, and became part of, other pictures. Eventually I was looking at these images and said to myself, "I'm just going to go get some mirrors!" So I went to Home Depot and got the biggest ones that would fit in my trunk. I was propping them up against chairs and tables and making photographs of my reflection as I moved through the space.

The most important aspect of the mirrors was that they offered a surface on which I could continue to organize that unwieldy accumulation of laser printouts, of unresolved material I had carried with me from New York. What you are not seeing in this exhibition, of course, are the early, informal, and more casual, experimental snapshots that preceded the eventual formal compositions. In *STUDIO WORK*, the background of the ever-changing studio space became the repeating element in the series as the subjects, figures, and objects at the center of the pictures cycled in and out. At UCLA, with the mirrors, I initially envisioned their surfaces as holding the unbundled printouts, temporarily organized by my own associations, with a reflected background of the studio (and my own reflection behind them) that would

Fig. 3
Paul Mpagi Sepuya
Self-portrait with Matija
2010
Archival inkjet print
Courtesy the artist

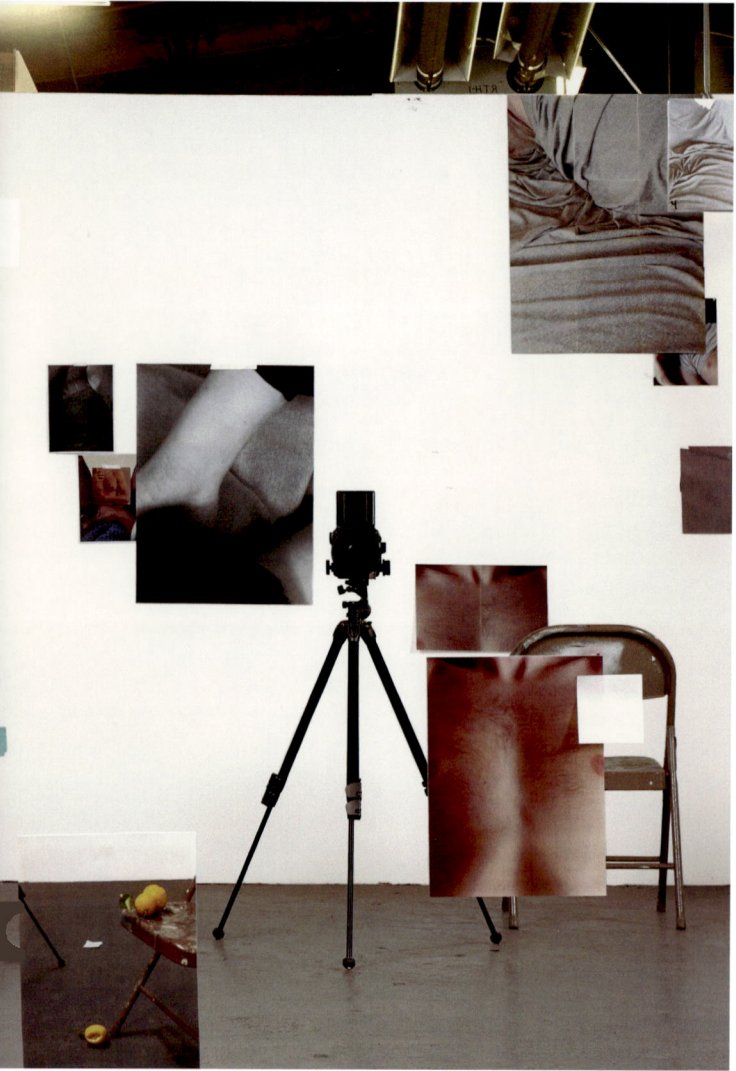

become a repeating, but gradually changing, site. The material would be organized, photographed, bundled, and eventually turned into later volumes of *Some Recent Pictures.*

So the fragmentation in the 2015 *Studies* is a result of that letter-size-paper printout material, some of which has become part of the following volumes of *Some Recent Pictures*. But I realized I needed to work with another kind of fragmentation that was more accountable to me, my hand, etc. So that's where the kind of cutting and tearing and "collaging" on the mirror surface comes in, in the project *Figures, Grounds and Studies* [2016–17]. *Figures* were the portraits, *Grounds* were both the site of the studio and the tropes of the studio, and then *Studies* were the reworking of things on the mirror's surface [fig. 4].

Fig. 4
Paul Mpagi Sepuya
Study for T.H. with Three Figures (0707)
2015
Pigment print on dibond with wood bracing and blocks
Courtesy the artist

WA Smudges, dust, fingerprints are all part of the residue accumulated on the mirrors you use to make many of your photographs. When you started using mirrors, did you always intend to keep the traces of touch on the mirror surface, or did that come later?

PS The smudges in the first mirror studies were left as an indication that the mirror's surface was not intended to be a trick "non-space," and because I intended every image to be direct about its making. The metaphors extending from the latency versus visibility emerged later.

Darkroom Mirror Study (_1990750) [2016, page 79] is the first successful attempt at photographing a mirror surface in the space of the "dark room." It can be thought of as an opposite to A Ground (File0083) [2015, page 65], which depicts a mirror turned at a slight angle, reflecting the studio walls and some gold drapery off scene. But at the center of that mirror is a body-print smudge of my friend Evan, who sat in the scene for a portrait. He discusses that image in his contribution to this book. This was the outtake, an aftershot that held a lot of interest for me, because the trace was present yet invisible. Latent. So I became interested in photographing the smudges, the smears, and the traces that are left on the surface of the mirrors, and are mostly rendered invisible or obliterated against the reflected white walls of the studio.

And this is where it gets into the whole play of the darkroom. This is the idea that a latent image or trace is made visible through a process within or against darkness or dark material. It requires this dark black and brown fabric, or black camera apparatus, or my black body to make these otherwise invisible—or rendered invisible—traces visible. And so I realized that in order to actually get a photograph of the traces, I had to construct a dark cloth around the mirror, and I could move behind the backdrop into this space.

And it's in this space that I have continued to work, in front of, straddling, and behind the backdrop and props that construct the photographer's studio. The backdrop delineates a space that is intended to be seen, to be background to a subject, but by extension also creates a space that is *not* meant to be seen. And it is in this space that the otherwise invisible is rendered visible again. I love the analogies to the photographer's darkroom; the social darkroom of sexual-social encounters. The flipping of the priorities of light and clarity in photography on their heads. I find so much potential to keep working in this space.

Grease on Glass
Evan Moffitt

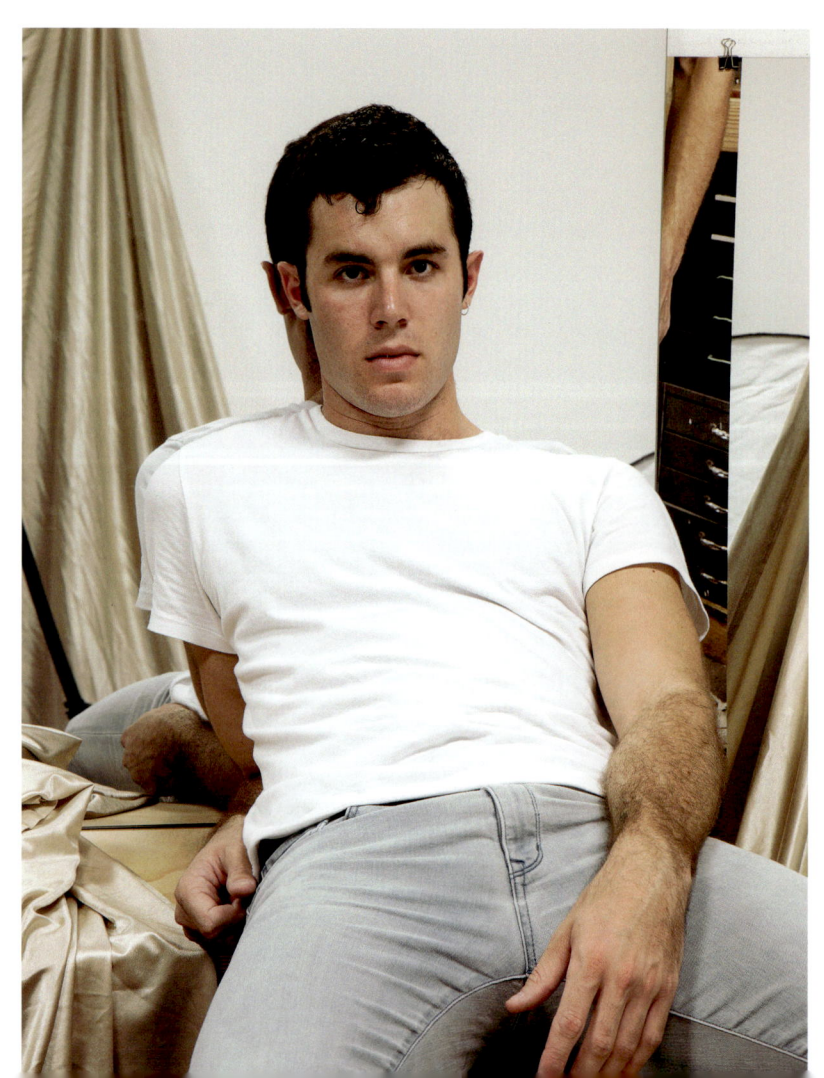

1.

A young man slouches against a mirror. A boy almost, his pale face smooth as the surface of the glass, his unwashed curls and crisp white t-shirt are the marks of a 1950s greaser. But the denim is cheap and stretchy, and a single hoop hangs from his left ear. His face seems about to turn, the brows inching slightly toward a furrow.

I try to recognize myself in the photograph (fig. 1) when I see it for the first time, behind glass, framed and mounted to a sheet of Visqueen. After the initial shock of confrontation in the brightly lit gallery of The Artist's Institute in New York, on an afternoon in the spring of 2016, I wonder what I'm doing there—or rather, what my portrait by the artist Paul Mpagi Sepuya is doing in a show curated by the writer Hilton Als, exhibited next to a bust of James Baldwin. But the longer I look, the less of myself I see. Not the double of my present self, weary and unshaven, but a portrait of a boy at the very moment he's being split in two. The mirror fractures his body so that a second profile, similar but not equal to the first, emerges Janus-like behind him. There, in that mirror space, his double's arm stretches out toward a shiny beige curtain that seems to belong to a different universe entirely, while the black leg of a metal tripod strikes his knee, anchoring him in the moment of bifurcation. I wonder which way is forward and which is back.

I first sat for Paul the week before I moved to New York from LA, the city where we had met. The city where we were both born and raised. He was working in the UCLA graduate studios, a white-washed warehouse with vaulted ceilings by one of the dry Culver City drainage channels, where aloe and oleander poke through in scrubby patches. I had never sat for a portrait before—not a *real* one, anyway, by a photographer who could capture deep emotional registers in blank faces. Whose pictures showed that blankness was an impossibility.

Paul set up the box on which I sat, then placed one mirror, and another; he clipped up scraps of old prints to their surfaces. There were tons of these scattered on the studio floor, cut up limbs and shreds of embroidered fabric—a scene of the quiet violence that marks the creative act, which must destroy in order to achieve perfection. A sliver of a man's arm, pale and veiny, hangs beside my head in the final image, photographed in front of flat file cabinets. Later, as I looked at the picture in the gallery, I remembered wondering if I, too, would become a scrap, my limbs woven through the portraits of other men, or stored like a cadaver in that same flat file. My picture isn't for me, I know, but for people who will see me without us ever meeting. It testifies to an intimacy between strangers made possible by the relationship between artist and subject, friend and photographer, that will constitute an archive of human contact. An archive, in short, of Paul's community.

2.

I don't know all these men, who pose languidly in bed, nude or mostly so, in the portraits Sepuya made in the years after he moved to Brooklyn in 2002—though I'm often haunted by his images of my friends and former lovers, which seem to appear everywhere I go. Rafi, Marques, Devin, Ben are strangers to me. Pericles is a friend, and yet I don't recognize his sultry gaze in his photograph (page 30) when I first

Fig. 1
Paul Mpagi Sepuya
A Portrait (File0085)
2015
Archival pigment print
Courtesy the artist

encounter it in 2019, eleven years after it was taken. (If the camera sees what the eye cannot, it's only the photographer's vision that ultimately reaches us.) Sepuya began documenting his friends, mostly queer men of color who lived near him in Brooklyn, in the years just before and after the financial crisis, often convening at Metropolitan Bar and, a few years later, at The Spectrum. Everything felt precarious in those days, with student debt and unemployment rising like the empty glass condo towers that had begun to obscure Williamsburg's view of Manhattan. Sepuya's photographs expose a scene that felt like it could splinter, even as it affirmed his identity as an artist and as a queer black man. The vulnerability in them is one that suggests deep love and trust, the kind that softens the eyes after sex. These photographs belong to a long stream of queer portraiture, from Carl Van Vechten's sensuous images of Harlem Renaissance performers, to Peter Hujar's piercing portraits of downtown New York figures, to the tender pictures of butches and bulldaggers by Catherine Opie, with whom Sepuya would later study at UCLA.

Sepuya's most regular subject is himself. Time and again he appears before the lens, aging indeterminately from picture to picture, in each of them clasping the remote shutter firmly in his hand. "Historically, the black literary tradition of auto-biography as self-creation and self-fashioning has been a necessary and radical act," the artist Thomas Allen Harris told his brother, artist Lyle Ashton Harris, in a 1994 interview.[1] People of color, especially those who are queer, have historically had little control over their own image. With his thumb on that black button, Sepuya claims his right to self-representation, making it easier for others, in turn, to claim their own.

The language of photography has always been one of domination. To capture a subject is to possess a part of them, frozen in silver gelatin or pixels. This is true, of course, of ethnographic photographs forcibly taken of enslaved people and colonial subjects; it is also true, in a different way, of the portraits of loved ones encased in lockets and wallet sleeves. The image escapes the body to which it once belonged and becomes a fetish; not a subjective representation, but an object to study and caress. To trim, fold, and even tear.

When Sepuya moved back to Los Angeles in 2014, he began to subject his own image to such tender little acts of violence. Misprints were ripped up and arranged into abstract collages with the discarded edges of photographs that already littered the studio floor, and then taped to the surface of a wall-mounted mirror. Some self-portraits were blown up life-size, printed out on sheets of A4 paper, and pieced together like faded tiles that fail to neatly match. Repeatedly throughout the *Mirror Studies*, Sepuya's own body becomes fragmented, knotted up with the indeterminate limbs of other subjects with whom he's posed. These are not images of self-creation but rather of dissolution. Baroque whorls of flesh—dark and pale, smooth and hairy—recall what Leo Bersani once described as the ego's "self-shattering"[2] in the act of passive gay male sex, best invoked (if metaphorically) by Caravaggio's many scenes of religious ecstasy.[3] Baroque art seems as apt a reference for these constructions as it does for Sepuya's more recent *Dark Room* portraits, suffused with chiaroscuro. Submission to the will of God becomes a subversive surrender to the pleasures of the body.

The folds of drapery behind these models open us onto illicit views, while Sepuya's hand reaches from outside the frame to hold the photographic fragments in place. In *Mirror Study (0X5A0486)* (2017, fig. 2), for instance, his fingers poke out every-where, probing the chest and thigh of an unidentified man like Doubting Thomas, who must touch in order to believe. They indicate what Kobena Mercer called "the messy spaces in-between the binary oppositions that ordinarily dominate representations of difference."[4] Sepuya's fingers and limbs fuse to the broken bodies of white men in a web of race and desire that cannot be untangled.

Mercer wrote those words in his quintessential essay, "Mortal Coil" (1998), when confessing his uneasy attraction to Robert Mapplethorpe's *Black Book* (1986).[5] It seems fitting that on the table in *STUDIO WORK* (2010–11), Sepuya's only installation to date, sits Jack Fritscher's biography of Mapplethorpe, *Assault with a Deadly Camera* (1994). The title says it all: rather than a reference to the S&M subculture Fritscher chronicles, it seems to refer to the way Mapplethorpe butchers black bodies with his camera frame, cutting them up like sides of beef. By rupturing his own body along with those of his subjects, Sepuya submits fully to the camera's assault, transforming the shutter click into a mutual and consensual *petite mort*.

3.

When I was eleven years old, my mother scolded me for leaving chalky lip marks on the bathroom mirror where I had kissed my own reflection. Hormones raging, I crossed my eyes as I stood on the counter, so my lover could emerge from the blur—not my pimpled reflection, but a body perfected by the mirror in ways I could only ever dream of. I didn't understand then that what I really desired was another boy.

Pigeons and locusts, Lacan wrote, fall in love with their own reflection, convinced that what they see is a potential mate. Humans, meanwhile, can't help but see a mirror for what it is. Why then, do we still let it tell us lies?

As Sepuya made increasingly self-conscious use of a studio mirror in his self-portraits, they began to resemble the more theatrical experiments of queer surrealist photographers for whom myth was closer to truth than to reality— the myth, most often, of Narcissus. See how Jean Marais gazes longingly at his reflection in Jean Cocteau's adaptation of another myth, *Orpheus* (1950)—a gesture echoed, four decades later, by Felix Gonzalez-Torres's twinned looking glasses, *Untitled (Orpheus, Twice)* (1991), a symbolic evocation of queer love and loss. Or how Charles Henri Ford gazes lustily at himself-as-odalisque in a 1936 self-portrait. As Richard Dyer has argued, such images are less about ego than homosexuality's problem of sameness and difference.[6] The mirror enabled queer photographers and filmmakers to depict men who loved other men, even when those other men were, on the surface, merely themselves.

How deep, then, must we dive into the mirror in order to encounter the Other? In Sepuya's photographs He is both on the surface and beneath it, layered in fragmented portraits that fail to be fully recognizable. "The mirror stage is a drama whose internal thrust is precipitated from insufficiency to anticipation," writes Lacan, one "which manufactures for the subject, caught up in the lure of spatial identification, the succession of phantasies [sic] that extends from a fragmented body-image to a form of its totality . . . and, lastly, to the assumption of the armour of an alienating identity, which will mark with its rigid structure the subject's entire development."[7]

Fig. 2
Paul Mpagi Sepuya
Mirror Study (0X5A0486)
(detail)
2017
Archival pigment print
Courtesy the artist and
DOCUMENT, Chicago

A reflection in a mirror is a perfect, depthless form, never as complex or shifting as the real body staring back at it. Sepuya chops up these reflections for us, refusing us neat or cohesive views. In his work, the mirror's imperfection enables us to see the imperfections within ourselves, further refracted by our relationships with others.

When I first visited The Spectrum, a since-shuttered club in East Williamsburg, Brooklyn, near where Sepuya used to live, I thought it was much bigger; the mirrored paneling on the walls doubled the crowd inside that dingy chamber, so its depths were difficult to ascertain. Maybe Paul felt the same way when he discovered it, a few years before I first arrived in New York City. By the end of the night, though, the looking glass would have vanished, fogged up and beaded with sweat. Its depth suddenly flattened, its horizon became a ground. Sepuya leaves us clues that his mirrors are really there: bits of black electrician's tape on their surfaces anchor us in space, like the nails Picasso and Braque painted onto their synthetic canvases. Lacan again: "the mirror-image would seem to be the threshold of the visible world."[8] The tape allows us to cross it.

Smudges, too, invite us in. Sepuya's mirrors archive traces of bodies—fingerprints and fatty grease stains—the way the cut-up prints taped in layers to their surfaces archive his many photographic references. The *Dark Room* portraits constitute a record not simply of the body but *by* the body, one that hovers over the skin of the subjects we view through its filter, like the ghostly presence of a lover lately there.

4.

The next time I visited Paul's studio, he had moved to LA's Boyle Heights, not far from the old Art Deco Sears building. The space was filled with natural light he had come to depend on to make his work. While we caught up, I browsed through stacks of prints on the table and the books on his shelf—Moyra Davey and David Hammons catalogs, Virginia Woolf's *Orlando*. Before I knew it, our conversation became an impromptu shoot: I stood behind a sheet of peachy nylon and stretched it with my face and fingers while he snapped away. When Paul paused to review the images on his camera, I sat down on a wooden box—the same one, I imagined, I'd sat on two years earlier—and leaned against a mirror. Paul noticed that my body left a fog of heat on the glass, and he asked me to stay there while he set up a black curtain to enclose us. In the final image, I'm lifting up the corner of the curtain and looking in at Paul while he clicks the shutter, like a nineteenth-century photographer's assistant. As a critic, I wonder whether my voyeuristic presence implies invitation or intrusion. Paul and I are, seemingly, locked in Mercer's mortal coil, an imbrication of eroticism and race, whose mutual disavowals only deepen their codependency. I am, at once, a curious friend, a lover, and a spy.

Later that afternoon, after I had left, more friends arrived. The *Dark Room* portraits, unlike the *Mirror Studies*, show them whole: Malik Gaines, Vishal Jugdeo, Oscar Peña, A. L. Steiner. Queer bodies exposed in the spaces where they've often felt the safest and most free. The series is a direct pun on gay-bar sex rooms and the lab where photo negatives are developed, suggesting that the construction of a queer identity and the physical production of a photograph are parallel processes of self-creation, forged in the dark and brought to light. Again, we arrive at Harris's "necessary and radical act" at the very center of Sepuya's practice.[9]

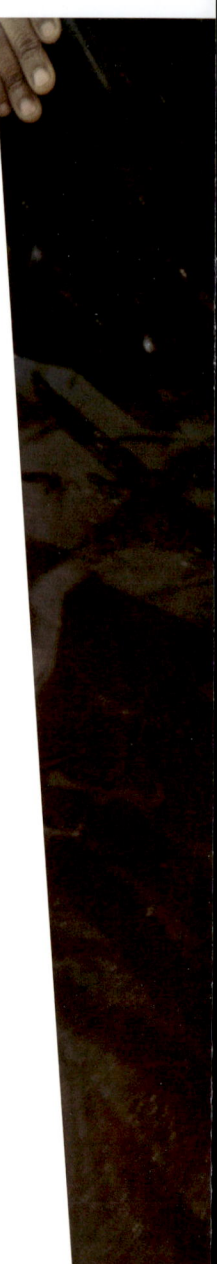

In each of these works, the camera's bionic eye serves both as silent witness and vanishing point. It is the only figure present in the twinned *Orifice (0X5A6982)* (2018, fig. 3 and page 89) and *Aperture (_2140020)* (2018, page 88), filling a single hole cut from a curtain in the former, but ironically missing from the same hole in the latter. A device designed to capture light serves as a plug for a place where the sun don't shine. And yet, pressed to the glory hole Sepuya has cut, the camera is also a voyeur: instead of simply reproducing the (gay) male gaze, it directs it piercingly at us. If in *Aperture (_2140020)* the curtain, like a bathroom stall, is a shield that saves us from overexposure—a quality that fittingly frays the velvety richness of these photographs' black—then in *Orifice (0X5A6982)*, Sepuya refuses to grant us safety free of its consequences. Throughout his work, his subjects see as much as they are seen; he poses himself as much as he directs others to pose; and the camera impinges on our own presence, as viewers, as much as it grants us access to a world that was never ours, or never yours, to see.

Orifice (0X5A6982)* and *Aperture (_2140020)* are photographs reduced to their *punctum*, what Barthes called the "sting, speck, cut, little hole" of a composition.[10] In *Camera Lucida* (1980), the philosopher locates the punctum of an 1882 portrait of French explorer Pierre Savorgnan de Brazza, who colonized Congo and much of Central Africa, in a young black boy's hand resting on his inner thigh.[11] Homoeroticism, race, and power prick the history of photography all over. Sepuya sees through these little cuts—apertures onto which the self, and the culture that conditions it, unfold.

5.

There's a third portrait of me (page 65), one in which I don't appear. Or rather, it resembles my first portrait, but the box is empty; I seem to have never arrived. I first encounter it on display in *Being: New Photography 2018* at The Museum of Modern Art, New York, and it appears again in Sepuya's 2019 solo exhibition at the Contemporary Art Museum St. Louis. Its mirror reflects nothing back but the studio wall, and the fleshy curtains draped along its sides. I can't help but intuit a bodily presence the way I do with *Orifice (0X5A6982)* and *Aperture (_2140020)*. The punctum here is that very backdrop which enables Sepuya, and all his subjects, to see ourselves as we are. As he reveals us to be.

Endnotes

1. Lyle Ashton Harris and Thomas Allen Harris, "Black Widow: A Conversation," in *The Passionate Camera: Photography and Bodies of Desire*, ed. Deborah Bright (Routledge: London, 1998), 249.
2. Leo Bersani, *Is the Rectum a Grave? And Other Essays* (University of Chicago Press: Chicago, 2010), 25.
3. Leo Bersani and Ulysse Dutoit, *Caravaggio's Secrets* (MIT Press: Boston, 1998), 87.
4. Kobena Mercer, *Welcome to the Jungle: New Positions in Black Cultural Studies* (1994), p. 173, quoted in *The Passionate Camera: Photography and Bodies of Desire*, ed. Deborah Bright (Routledge: London, 1998), 94.
5. Kobena Mercer, "Mortal Coil: Eros and Diaspora in the Photographs of Rotimi Fani-Kayode," in *Overexposed: Essays on Contemporary Photography*, ed. Carol Squiers (New Press: New York, 1999), 196.
6. Richard Dyer, *Gays and Film* (British Film Institute: London, 1977), 67ff.
7. Jacques Lacan, *Écrits: A Selection* (W. W. Norton & Co: New York, 1977), 4.
8. Ibid.
9. Harris and Harris, *The Passionate Camera*, 249.
10. Roland Barthes, *Camera Lucida: Reflections on Photography* (Farrar, Straus & Giroux: New York, 1980), 24.
11. Ibid., 52.

Fig. 3
Paul Mpagi Sepuya
Orifice (0X5A6982) (detail)
2018
Archival pigment print
Courtesy the artist and
team (gallery, inc.)

Plates
Early Portraits

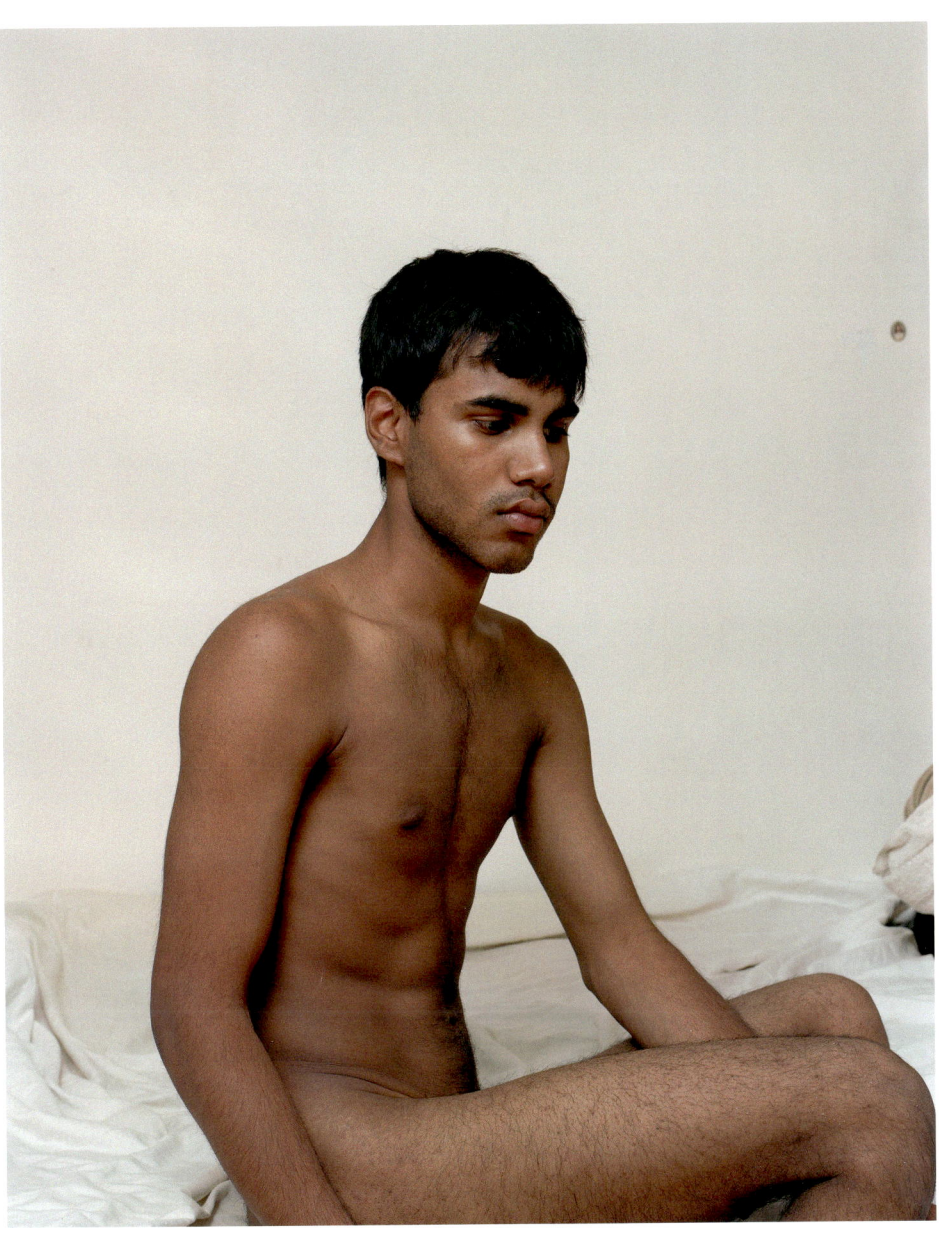

Rafi, 2005

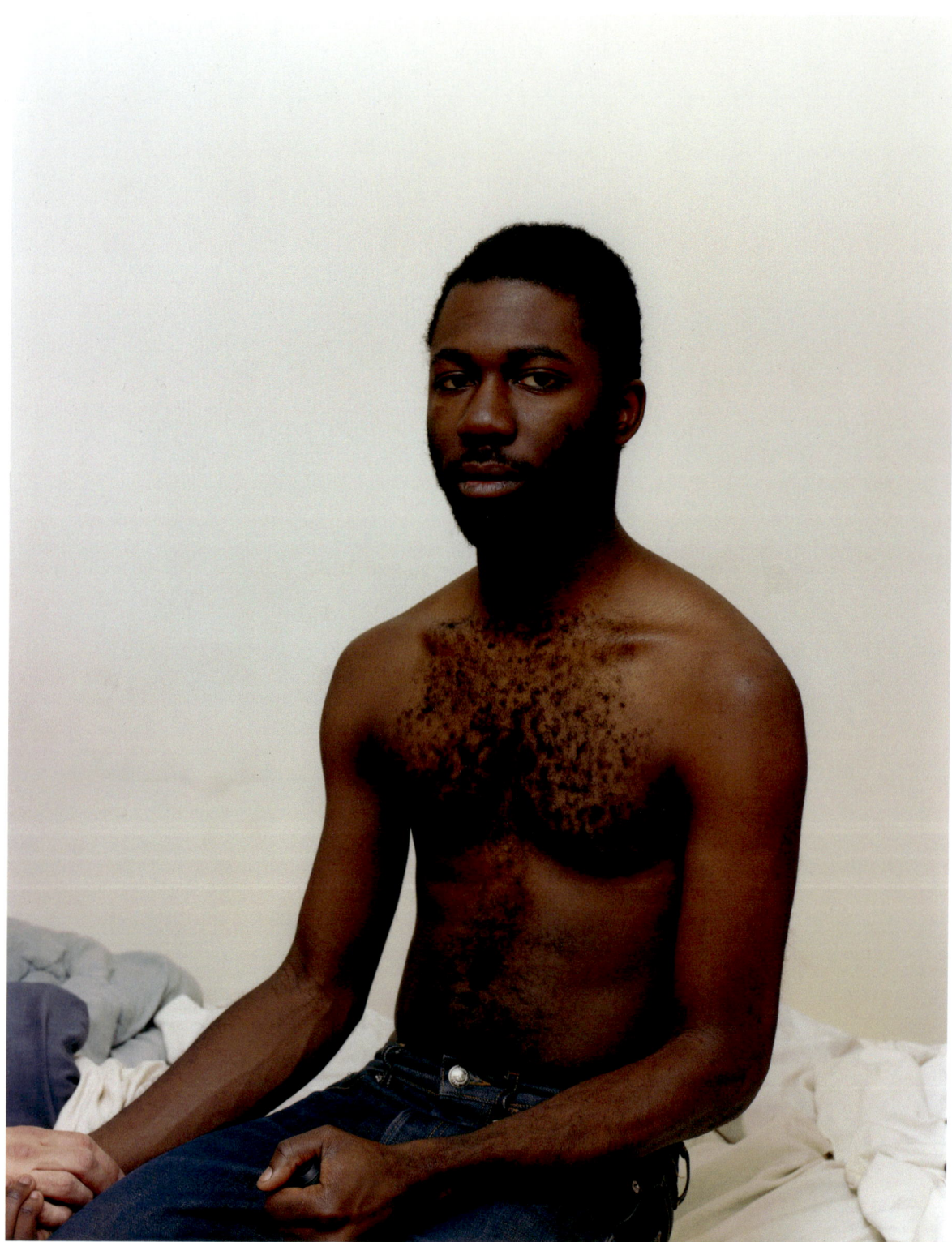

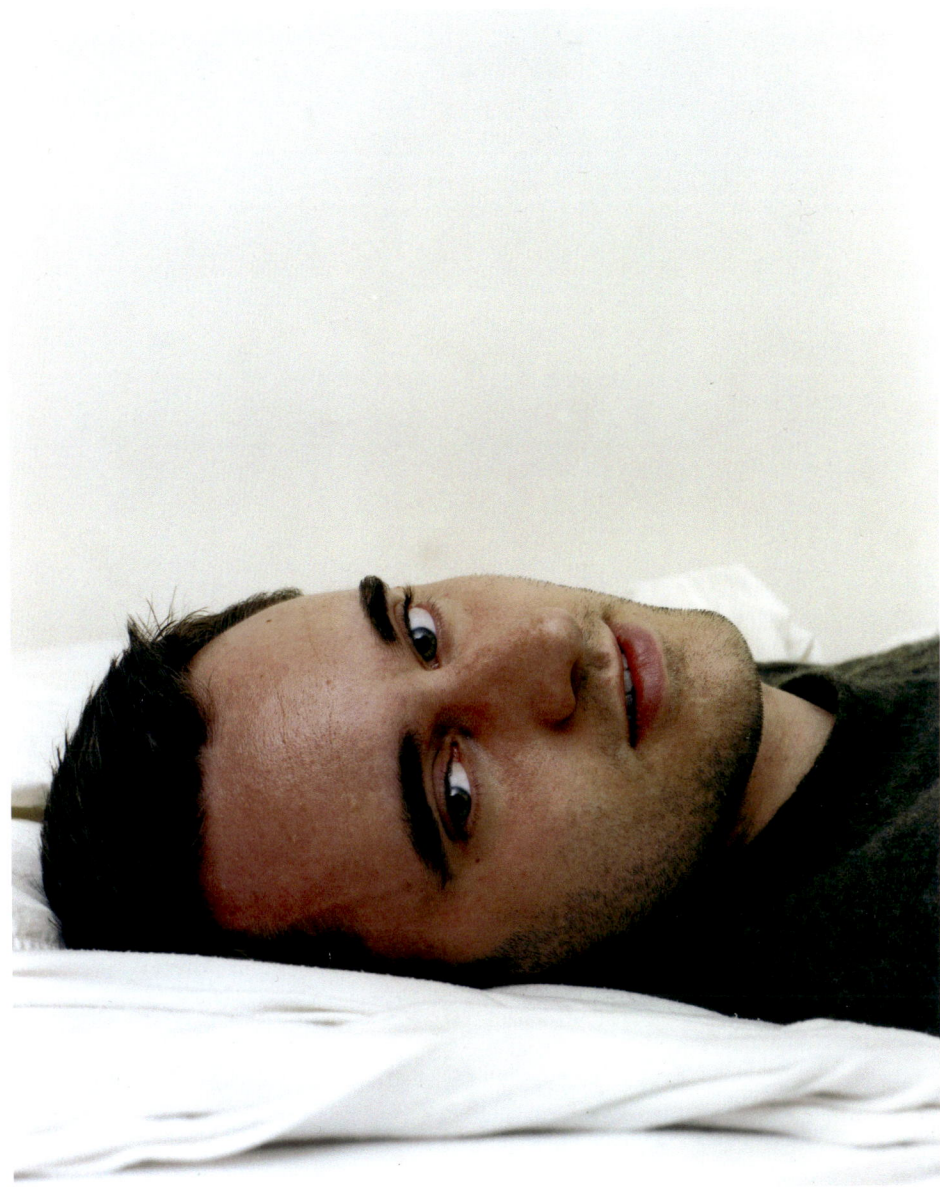

Self Portrait Holding Joshua's Hand, 2006

Tyler, 2008

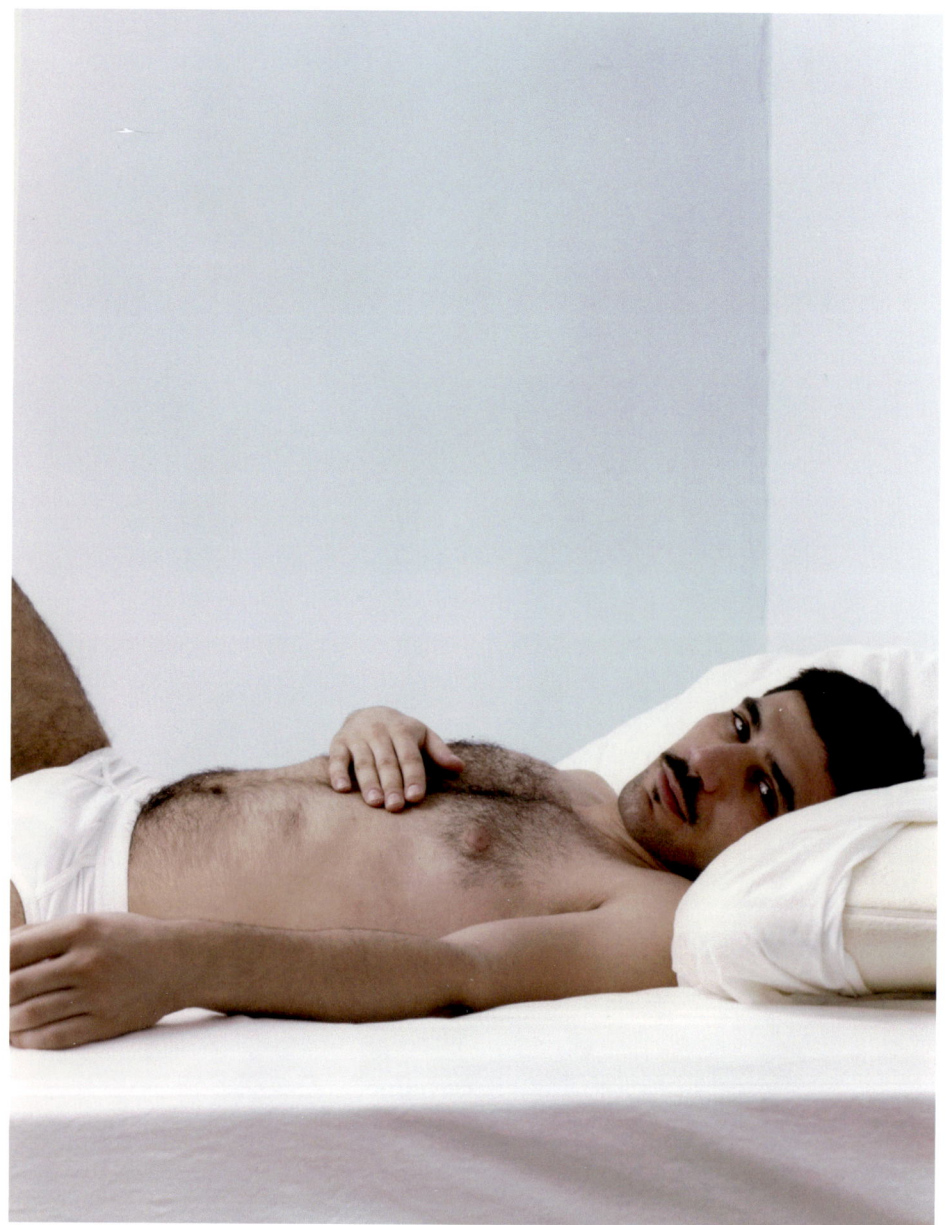

Pericles, 2008

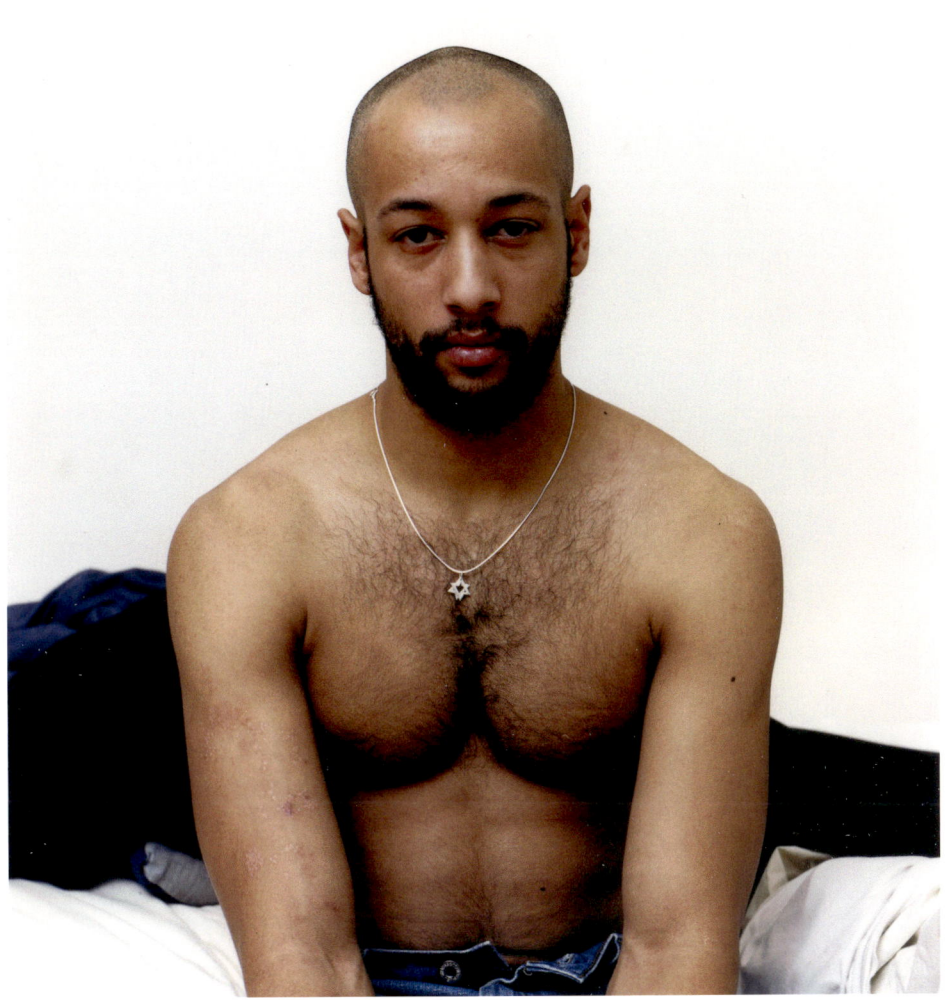

Devin, 2008

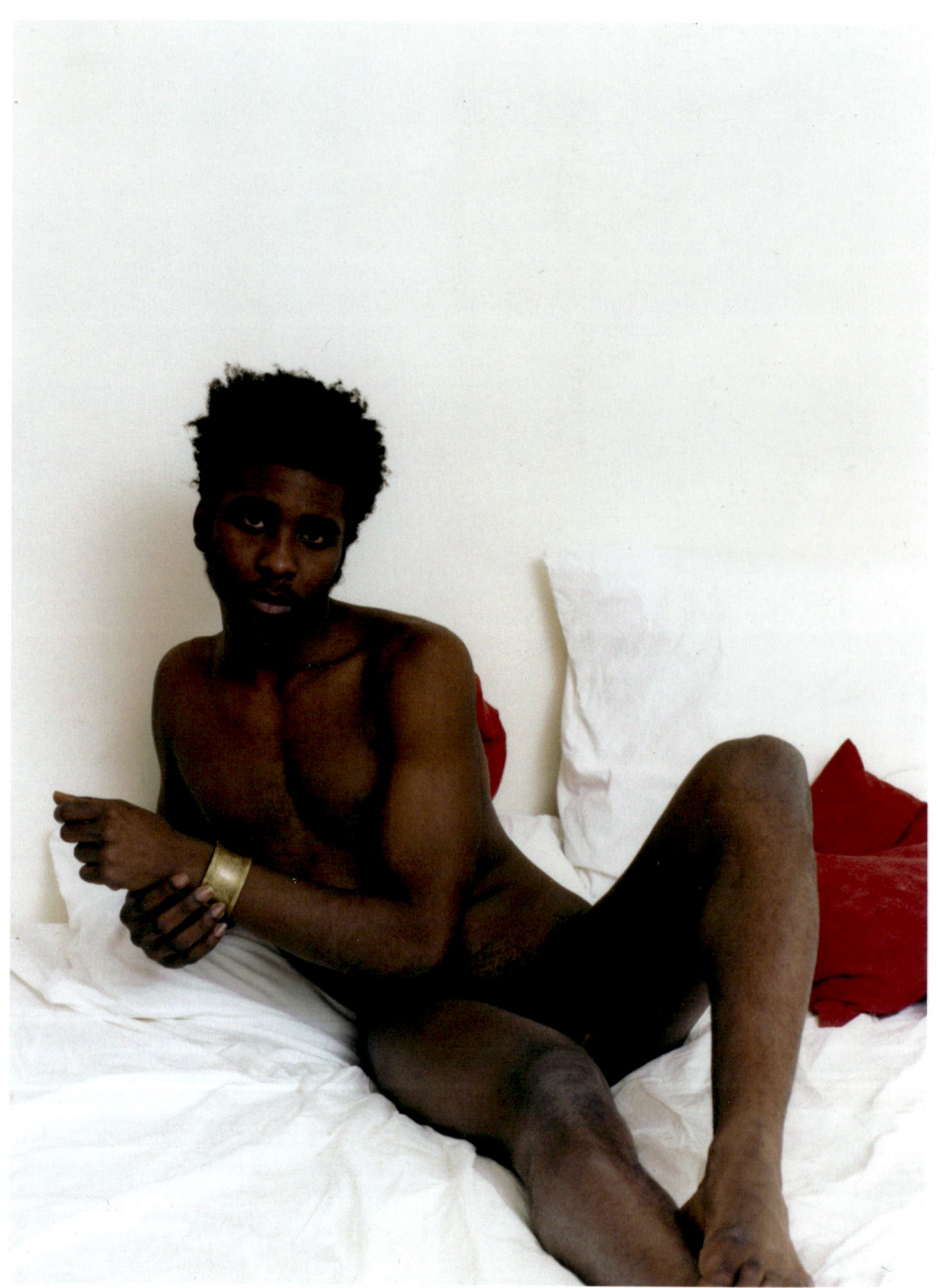

Marques (Adriano, Marques, Henning), 2008

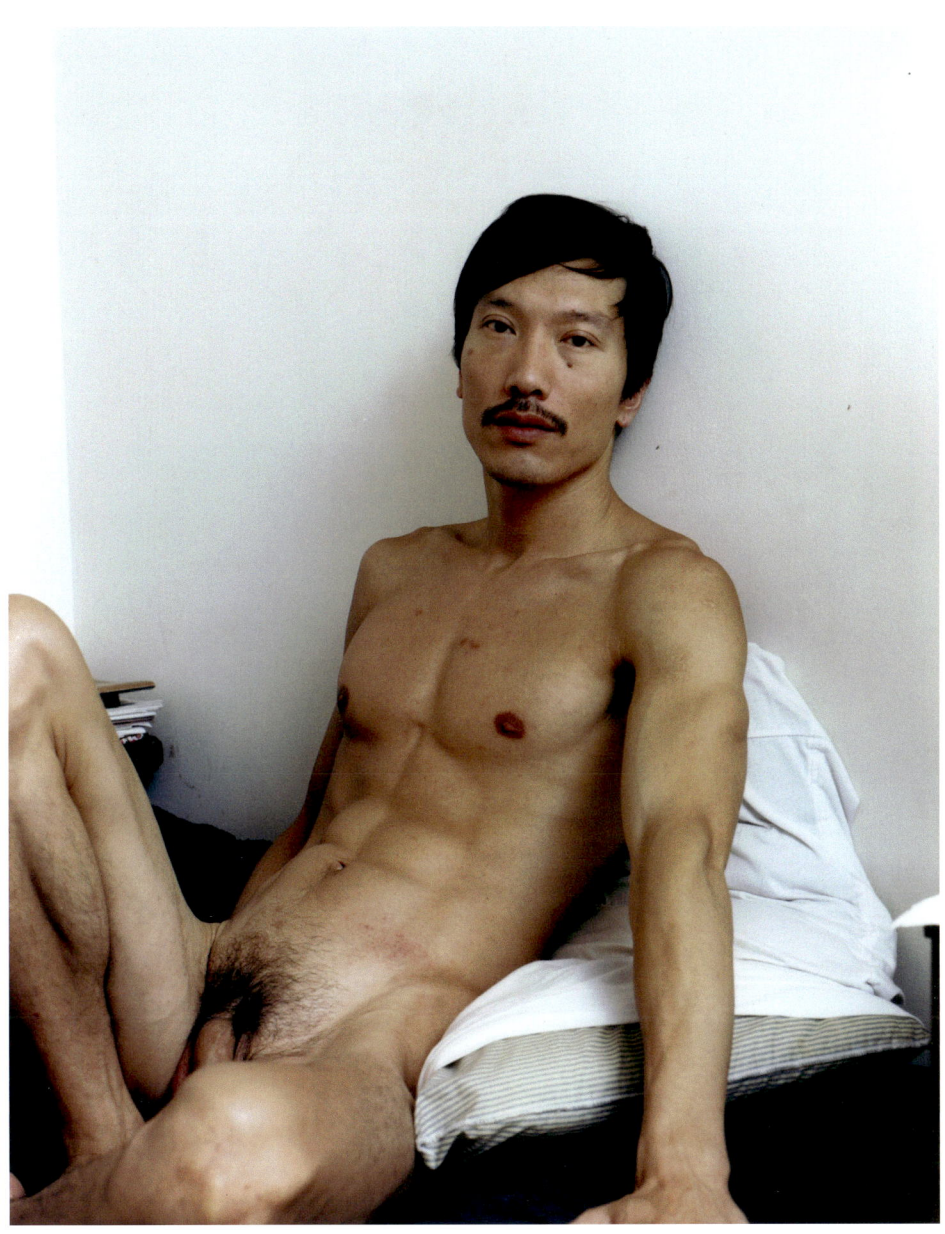

Ben, 2009

Fragments of red-hued photographic paper form a jagged layer of imagery in Paul Mpagi Sepuya's *Studio Wall (_1000021)* (2018, page 60), crisscrossing the composition like dramatic peaks of a landscape, or flames shooting up from the bottom of the frame. Much of the imagery on these fragments is drawn from iPhone snapshots made by the artist in bars and clubs. The specific shades of red—rusty, burnt—are not the result of gels, or of color modifications in development, but instead come from bar lights cast onto bodies inhabiting the dark interiors. For Sepuya, this color also points to the process of the photographs' production: "It's the red-orange of the photographic darkroom and the late night darkroom."[1] In this way, these red paper strips refer to the circumstances of their own making in a manner that is at once evocative and material, and they do so amidst a constellation of other sources—studio photographs and iPhone pictures shot by the artist, installation views of his work presented in exhibitions, and a diverse array of appropriated images—all printed on pieces of photographic paper layered upon and next to one another, like so many collected scraps tacked onto a studio wall. Together the presence of all these sources raises complicated questions about the work itself: How and where was it made, and who was involved? Are the relationships between these players readily legible, or are they hidden?

    Or, are they coded? On the surface, the relationships are visible for any viewer to observe, but their nuances may not be fully decipherable. Tucked into the bottom left corner of *Studio Wall (_1000021)*, for example, Sepuya has included a slice of a 1934 photograph by Cecil Beaton that depicts the artist Pavel Tchelitchew standing before a canvas, his palettes and brushes on a cart directly to his left (fig. 1). Missing in Sepuya's crop of the photograph is the subject of Tchelitchew's painting: Peter Watson, art patron (and object of Beaton's affection). At first glance, the photograph appears to be one that Sepuya has referenced elsewhere, but closer inspection reveals that Beaton made two distinct photographs of Tchelitchew in the midst of this painting. In the first, there are only two figures pictured; in the other (fig. 2), a third joins them: Tchelitchew's partner Charles Henri Ford. Across the two images, Tchelitchew himself appears to be simply lifted from one context of his studio to another, like a form cut out from the paper (in the manner of Sepuya's own photo scraps), with his identical pose, rolled-sleeved jacket, and direct over-the-shoulder gaze. As Sepuya has described the latter photograph and his own work, "In Beaton's and my triple portraits are laid bare those series of relationships between the makers and patrons, subjects and desirers of images that are uniquely photographic. It is the

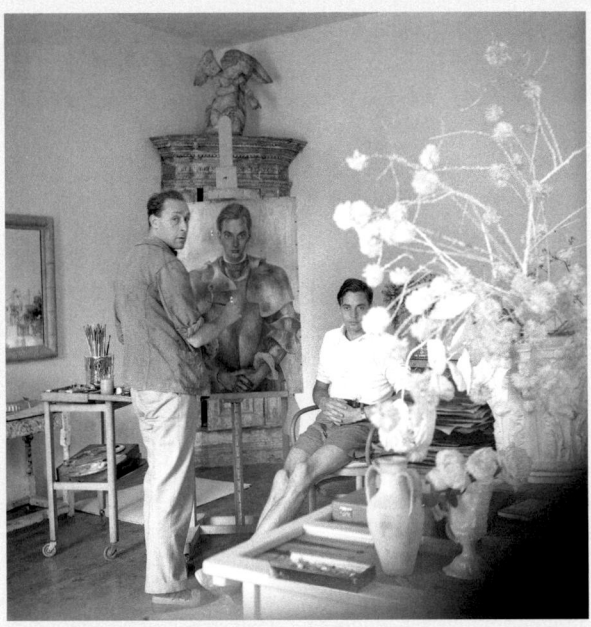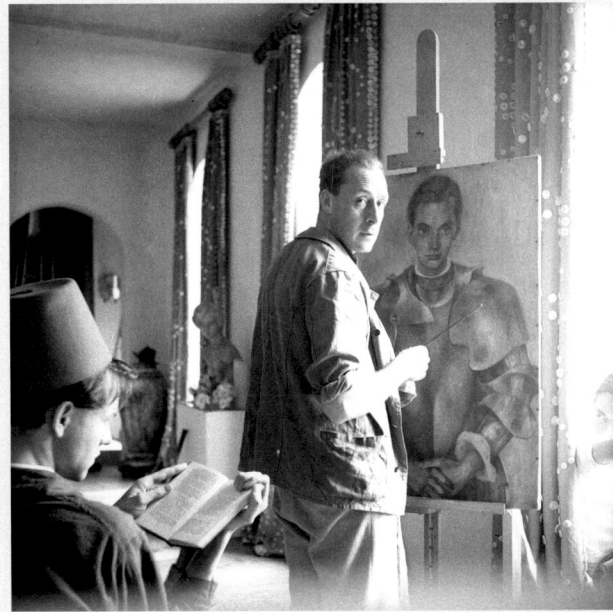

ability to simultaneously collapse disciplines, and interrupt discrete institutional knowledge through gossip that serves as an important historic marker."[2] This interruption is underscored by observing the two Beaton photographs next to one another: One may portray the "true" setting of the painting (with its even light and brushes sitting handy on the adjacent cart), but the other presents a more complicated picture of all the players.

Adjacent to the shards of deep red from the iPhone imagery, another lighter strip of predominantly red color in *Studio Wall (_1000021)* is comprised of rephotographed images, including reproductions of Henri Matisse's renowned painting, *The Red Studio* (1911). Matisse's composition (like Sepuya's) includes reproductions of his own artworks around the studio. These are represented through gleaming frames and multiple colors, while the walls themselves (which were actually white) are painted in a saturated red hue that seems to envelop the room. Indeed, the rest of the architecture and furnishings (a chair, a bureau, a grandfather clock) are only implied through outlines that the artist left unpainted—like the white gaps between the red curtains of photo paper in Sepuya's set of *Exposures* (2017, pages 86–87). This is an interior scene in which time is suspended, like the experience of the studio environment itself, and like so many of Sepuya's own studio compositions, in which all the components contained within have been flattened into one richly woven layer.

Winding our gaze clockwise from *The Red Studio*, at the very opposite corner of *Studio Wall (_1000021)* from Beaton's photograph, Sepuya has included a reproduction of Rotimi Fani-Kayode's *White Feet* (c. 1986–87), a square-format portrait of a recumbent male nude, his legs slightly crossed and the soles of his feet directed toward the viewer. The photograph appeared in Fani-Kayode's influential 1988 publication, *Black Male/White Male*. Although celebrating the black male body, the picture manifestly raises complications—of subjugation and idolization, of aestheticization of skin tones—within the portrayal of an artist's

Fig. 1
Cecil Beaton
Pavel Tchelitchew painting Peter Watson at Ashcombe
1934
Scanned from a negative/ digital file photograph
©The Cecil Beaton Studio Archive at Sotheby's

Fig. 2
Cecil Beaton
Charles Henri Ford and Pavel Tchelitchew painting Peter Watson
1934
Scanned from a negative/ digital file photograph
©The Cecil Beaton Studio Archive at Sotheby's

muse or sitter. The model's pose—prone on his stomach, vulnerable—echoes that of the young Tahitian girl in Paul Gauguin's 1892 painting, *Manaò tupapaú* (*Spirit of the Dead Watching*). It is also reminiscent of the reclining nude torso and legs depicted in a photograph made four decades prior by Minor White in San Francisco.[3] Both the Fani-Kayode and White photographs make appearances in an untitled collage by Sepuya included in a 2018 exhibition at The Museum of Modern Art (fig. 5). The principal figure in that collage is the artist himself, his camera lens nestled next to his hip, and his two bare feet tucked together at the base of his seated nude form. Unlike the white daybed employed by Fani-Kayode or Gauguin, Sepuya pictures his own body against a dark ground, perhaps a black velvet cloth, like those that appear regularly in both his portraits and White's. Indeed, White, who consistently interpreted photographs as reflections of an artist's own subjectivity (or, as he put it in a frequently cited letter to another photographer: "Your photographs are still mirrors of yourself"[4]), is an especially significant photographic ancestor within Sepuya's self-portrait collage.

And in and among the shards of photo paper, mirrors appear again and again in Sepuya's photographs, often without the viewer fully realizing their presence. Sometimes they reflect the camera apparatus itself; other times they confuse the representations of the artist and his subjects (which space does each figure inhabit?); most frequently they do all at once. Mirrors also play bystanding roles as studio props within the Beaton photographs referenced by Sepuya. They play more integral roles in a pair of photographs by George Platt Lynes, another vital chronicler of queer artistic circles. One image appears to be a simple portrait of

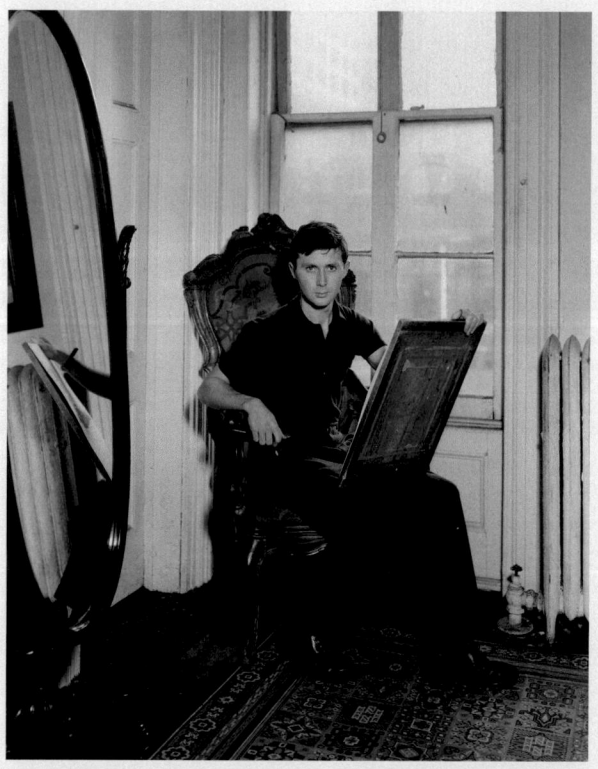
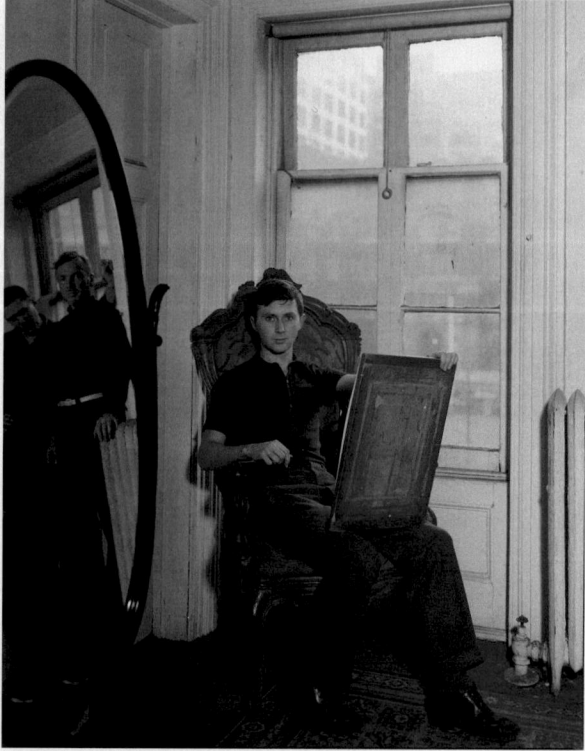

the artist George Tooker, holding a painting on his lap as he sits forward in his chair and locks his gaze with the camera (fig. 3). In the next picture, Lynes has shifted his perspective just slightly, so that the reflections of two other figures emerge in the adjacent mirror: artists Paul Cadmus and Jared French, longtime romantic partners and collaborators with whom Tooker was also involved (fig. 4).[5] These portraits in the trio's shared Greenwich Village studio space—where links are not always readily visible, even when they are present—are suggestive of the manner in which Sepuya has brought his own community into his studio and into his resulting work, both literally and metaphorically. Illustrations of works by artistic forebears share the frame with a range of material photographed by the artist (from studies made in the studio, to snaps of his friends at home, to views of "finished" works installed in exhibitions). All come together—or, to use Sepuya's words, all are simultaneously collapsed—within the studio.

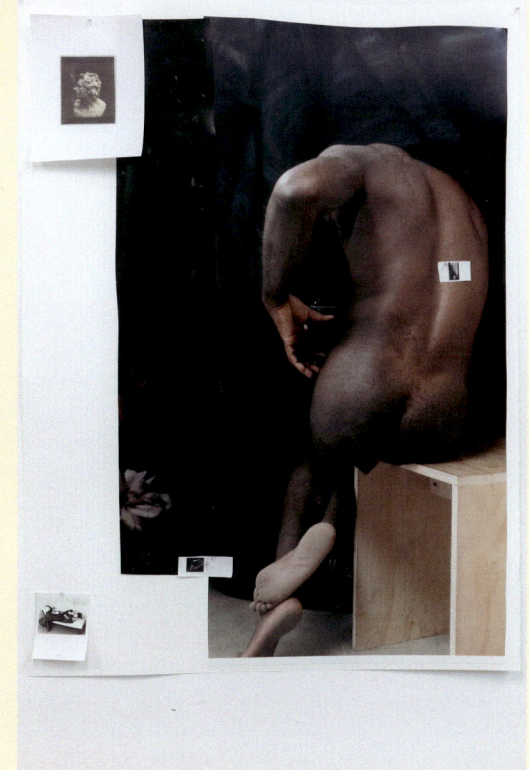

Endnotes

1. Correspondence with the artist, May 21, 2019.
2. Paul Mpagi Sepuya, "The Back Page," *Photograph* (September–October 2017), 128.
3. Like Matisse's *The Red Studio*, a print of this photograph is held in MoMA's collection—and the reproduction of the image that appears in Sepuya's collage was cut out from an illustrated museum checklist, further complicating the exchange between the studio, the archive, and the museum.
4. Minor White, "Letter to a photographer," November 1, 1962, in Peter C. Bunnell, *Minor White: The Eye That Shapes* (Princeton and Boston: Princeton University Art Museum and Little, Brown, 1989), 39.
5. For an illuminating reading of this triangle relationship, especially as illustrated via another photograph by Lynes of Cadmus, French, and Tooker in their studio, see Richard Meyer, "Threesomes: Lincoln Kirstein's Queer Arithmetic," in *Lincoln Kirstein's Modern* (New York: The Museum of Modern Art, 2019), 104–5.

Fig. 3
George Platt Lynes
George Tooker
1948
Gelatin silver print
The Museum of Modern
Art, New York
Gift of Russell Lynes
Image used with permission of The George Platt
Lynes Estate

Fig. 4
George Platt Lynes
George Tooker (with Paul Cadmus and Jared French)
1948
Gelatin silver print
The Museum of Modern
Art, New York
Gift of Russell Lynes
Image used with permission of The George Platt
Lynes Estate

Fig. 5
Paul Mpagi Sepuya
Untitled
2017
Pigmented inkjet prints
and laser prints on paper
Private collection;
promised gift on long-term loan to Minneapolis
Institute of Art
Courtesy the artist

Plates
STUDIO WORK
2010–11

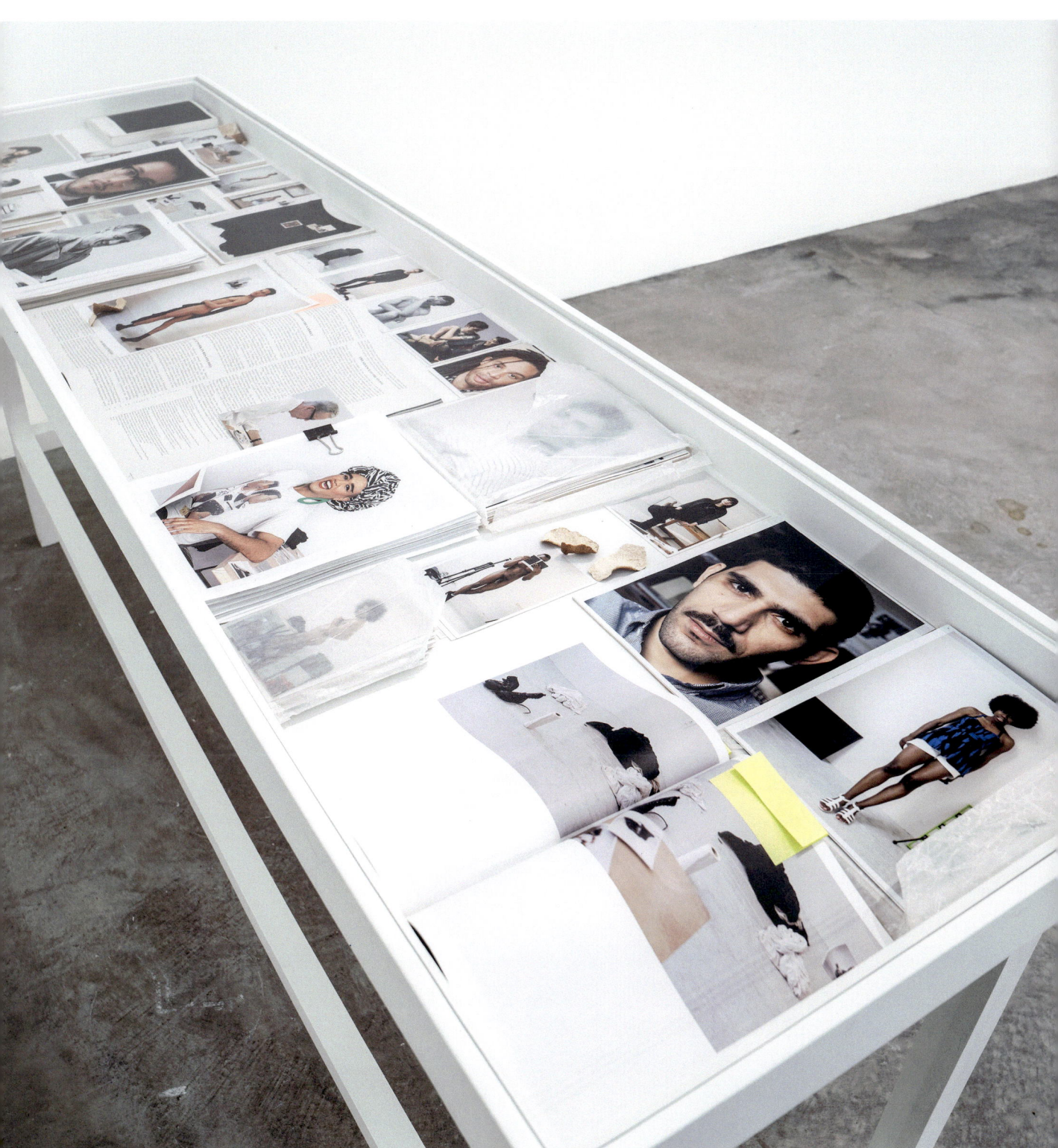

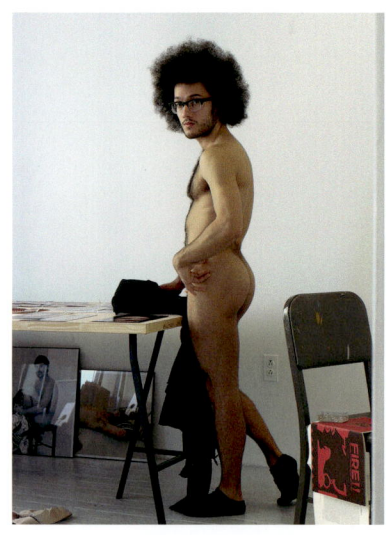

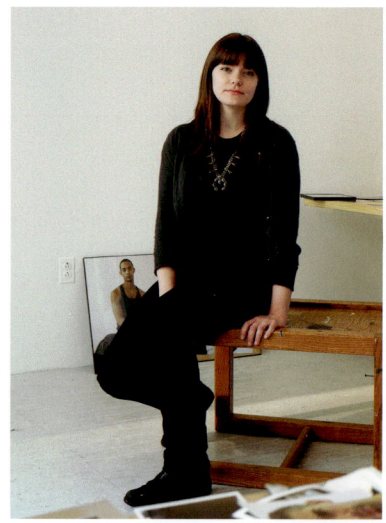

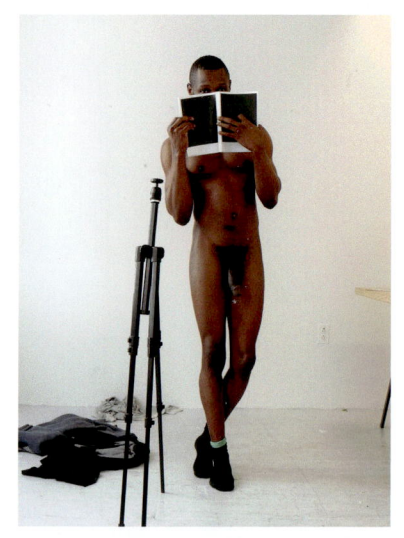

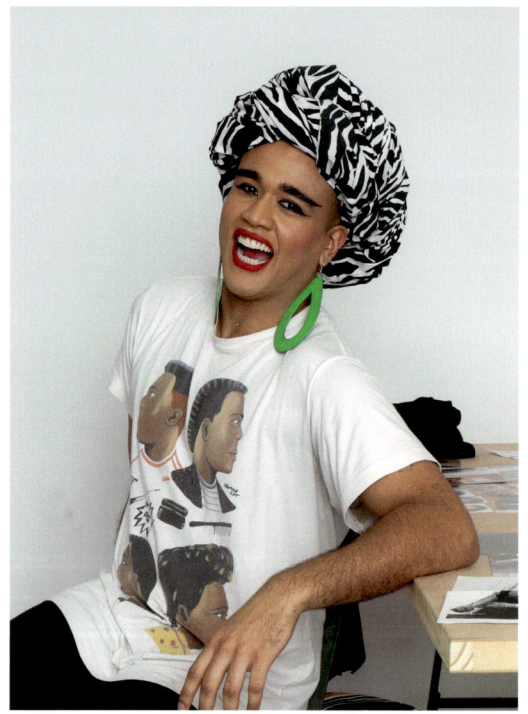

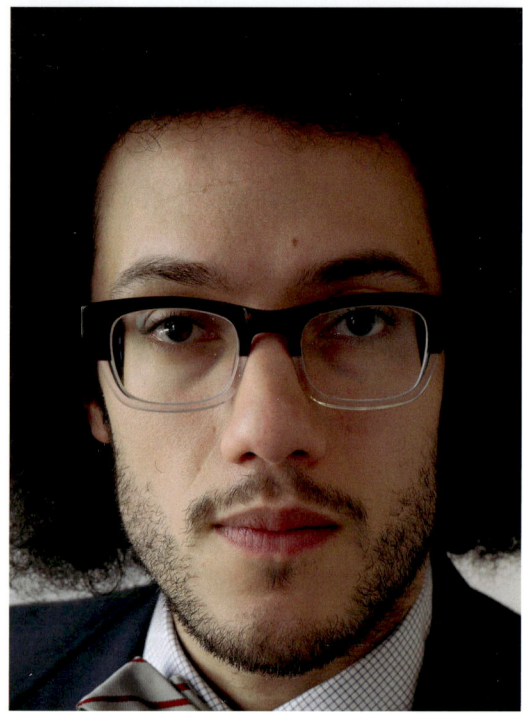

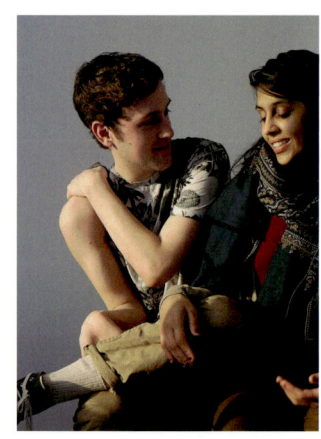

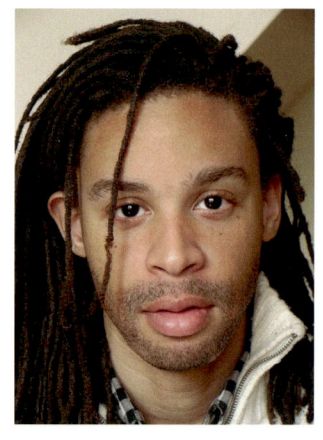

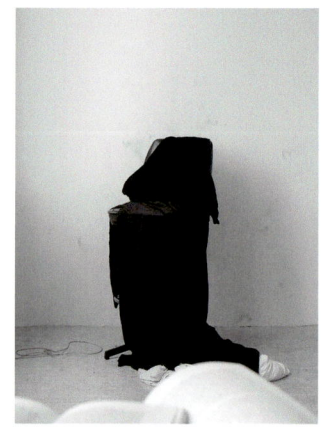

STUDIO WORK
(details),
2010–11

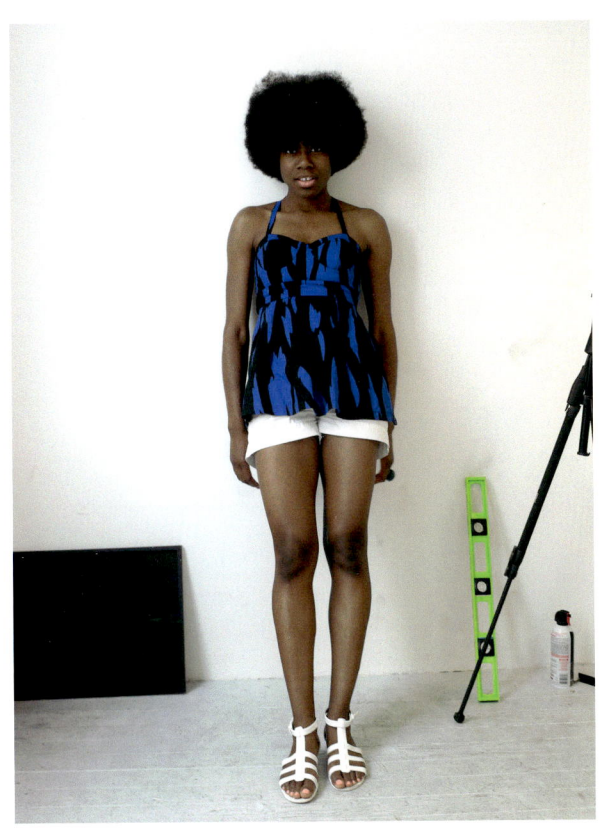

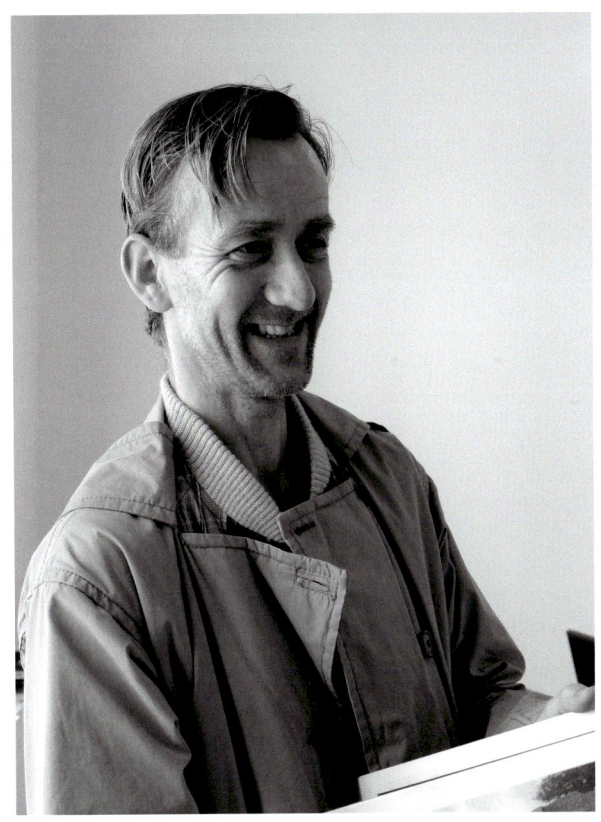

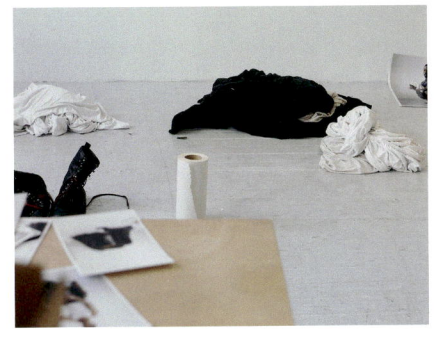

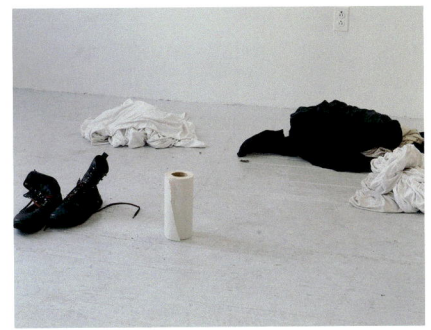

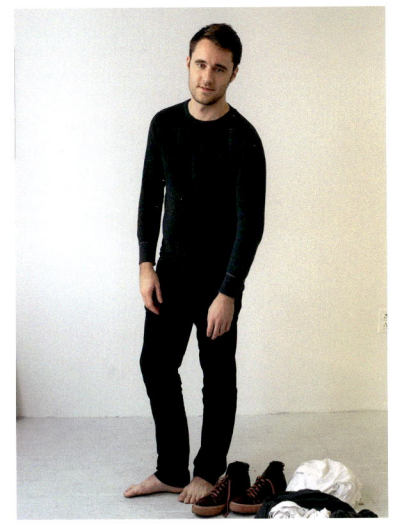

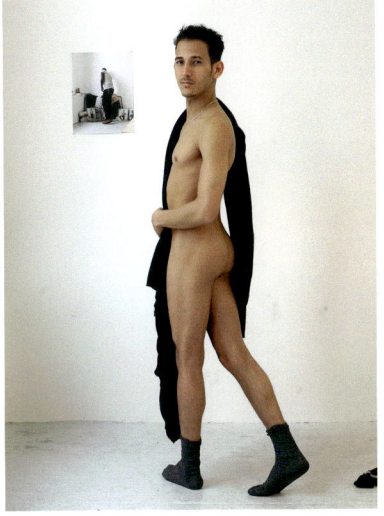

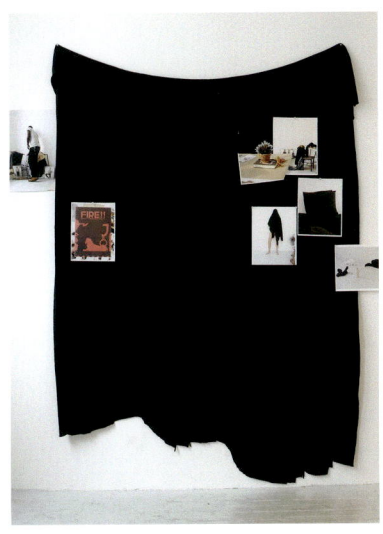

Darren, September 8, 2011

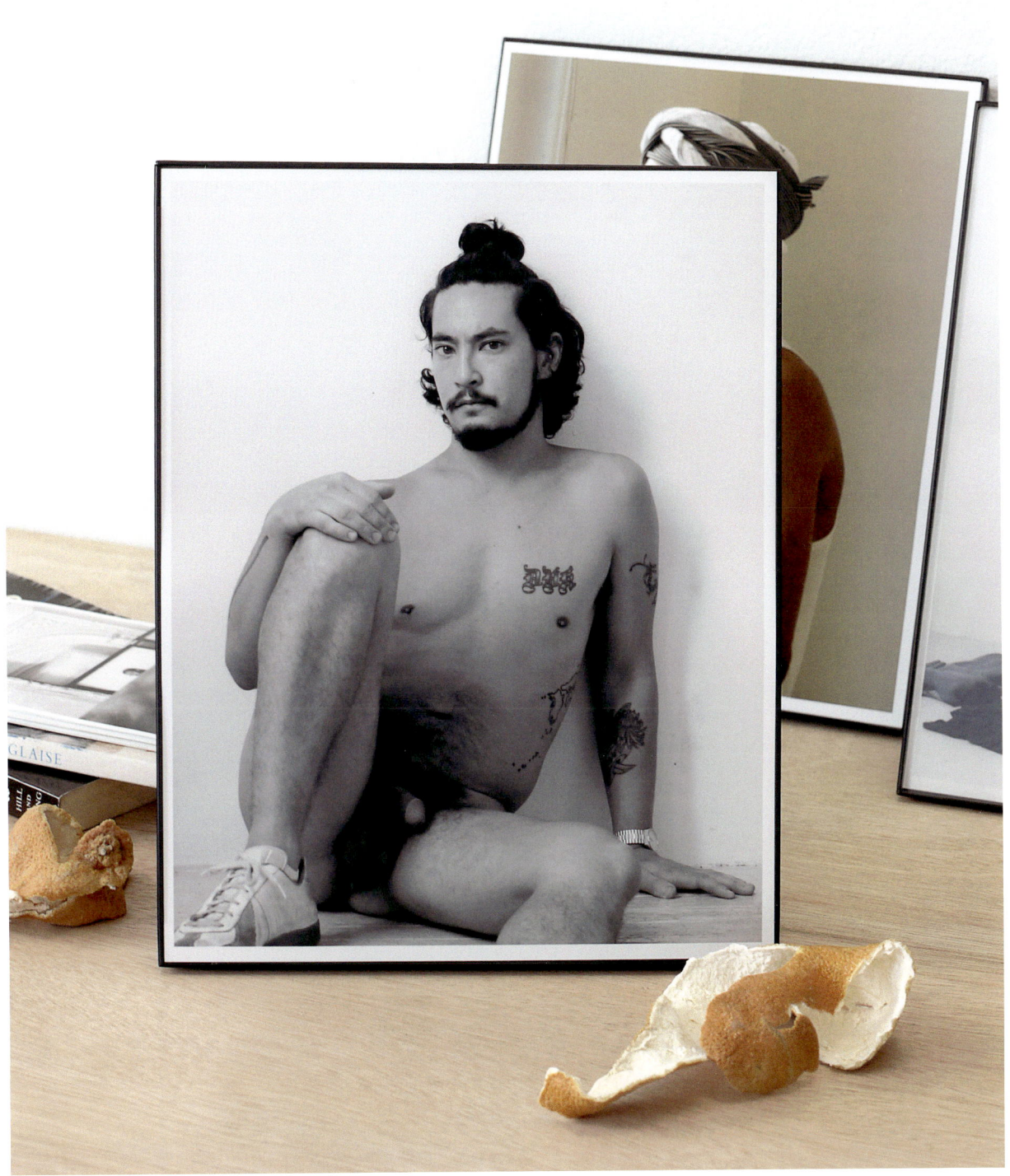

Barkley L. Hendricks's left arm bends at a 90-degree angle while holding a 35mm camera at eye level, away from his face. The photorealist painter (1945–2017) looks at himself with a humble attentiveness, sporting a trim beard and tall fedora. Hendricks's right hand rests in the V-shape where his white shirt opens. On a wall in Paul's studio, Hendricks stands facing a mirror in his own studio. Hendricks's self-portrait anchors a bulletin board-style collage that comprises Paul's photograph *Studio (_2150762)* (2017, page 61).

Other images collected in Paul's studio-wall collage include black image-makers, whether photographers or those using lower-tech media. The collection of images, grounded by pushpins, exceeds the edge of the frame, where viewers only catch a glimpse of the overlapping image. I learn from Paul that *Studio (_2150762)* documents a collection of images that feature black hands, cameras, or mirrors. A range of figures pose in beds and ad-hoc portrait studios. Amidst the intimate scenes are installation shots of Paul's own work, including tables and vitrines that have displayed these very images like reference points to histories of representation—as if to show them framed hanging on walls would disturb their private relationships. Such is Paul's commitment to the photographic medium as a fluttering infinity mirror of images in a field of inquiry.

Paul's work exudes a lustful skepticism of cameras and photographs. The studio-as-stage always reveals the backstage. The frame regenerates—from the macro level of presentation in exhibits, books, prints, and test strips—to propose every photograph made within the frame lives as an attempt at representation. Often the edges of the portrait studio, or the bulletin board of inspiration inside the studio, become the central focus to Paul's photographs.

The photograph and body, limb and fragment, incident and layer, learn to blur within Paul's art. The celebration of the incomplete image is found in the sequel to the image in the next shoot. In *Darren, September 8* (2011, page 43), an orange peel hardens like a watch against this photograph of other photographs, as if trying to pause the gesture of scrolling. Limitless memory cards rub against grainy negatives in the mixing of analog and digital. The stage and its cascade of images translate photography as an obsession that challenges the medium itself. Paul's work defies the illusory surface. He submits to the lens and reworks it.

Paul's studio in Los Angeles is a place to pose in front of time. With two tall-ceilinged rooms, skylights deliver an almost too-perfect bounty of California light, scoffing at the invention of the softbox. I open the door to a mirror against the wall facing a bench. To the right of the entrance is a library consisting of a

Fig. 1
Ariel Goldberg
Camera Lesson
2018
Inkjet print
Courtesy the artist

Fig. 2
Paul Mpagi Sepuya
with Ariel Goldberg
"Camera Lesson (_2210510)"
2018
Archival pigment print
Courtesy team (gallery, inc.)

pile of books on a wooden crate featuring Bauhaus photographers and 1980s gay painters, which may eventually become props.

Our friendship began in the Photography and Imaging Department at a university known for relentless privatization and real estate expansion. I have a fond memory of Paul helping me feed a roll of 35mm film onto metal reels. We swapped places in the light-sealed closet for loading film. All the plastic reels, designed in a more foolproof beginner's fashion, were in use. In the early aughts, when Paul was publishing work in *BUTT* magazine, I had a lawyer-to-be Jewish boyfriend. Daniel and I gave each other break-up gifts when I realized I was gay: I got a universal remote control on a keychain to turn off televisions at bars and he got a subscription to *The Economist*.

From the vantage point of my saturated queer trans life, I'm almost scandalized that I texted Paul to invite myself over for a studio visit because I was "in town for my ex-boyfriend's wedding." When Daniel greeted me at his *Aufruf* ceremony at an Orthodox synagogue in Beverly Hills, he was visibly nervous about how I would blend into the grand tradition of "men" and "women" sitting separately. The service was like a slow-motion crossing of the gender binary typical of public bathrooms. Instead of quick stares from eyes that might question a slight bulge in my chest as I move from stall to sink, I was ensconced in hours of familiar prayer without the English translation, staring at the view of the "women's side" from the "men's side."

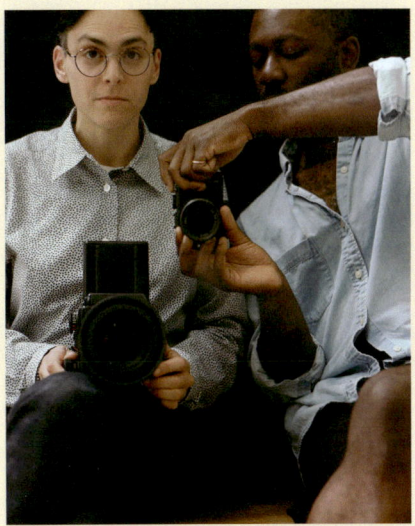

Paul generously listened to me recount the synagogue scene I had just escaped. Then we talked about the images of photographers (Paul included) holding their cameras, some of which appear in the aforementioned *Studio* and *Studio Wall* images—which may have been shot in the back nook of his studio, while music played from a large monitor and emails tumbled in; the mini fridge stocked with seltzer and iced coffee. Soon Paul's friend Clay showed up, who lounged in a Saturday odalisque pose on a nearby chair.

Paul tells me he has been inviting photographers to bring their cameras and take pictures with him inside his studio. The amateur quality of my phone left me unprepared. Paul offered his signature Mamiya RZ67.

As I sat on the bench and faced the mirror, I entered an alternate queer rite of passage with slightly more allure than the "men's side" at the synagogue. I paused as if looking around for the homoeroticism I associate with Paul's work. Then I kept my permeable aura of masculinity—my clothes—on. The unwieldy Mamiya RZ, not screwed onto a tripod, balanced on my knee, heavy in my hands. Paul sat next to me, the edge of my left arm and the edge of his right arm touching as he brought a handheld digital Fuji toward the mirror's reflection (fig. 2). By contrast, I glanced down to sharpen the image in the ground glass, then looked to the mirror for approval before alerting the emulsion (fig. 1).

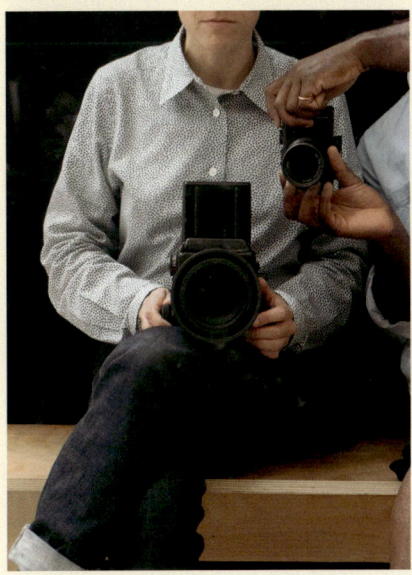

Plates
Some Recent Pictures
2013–14

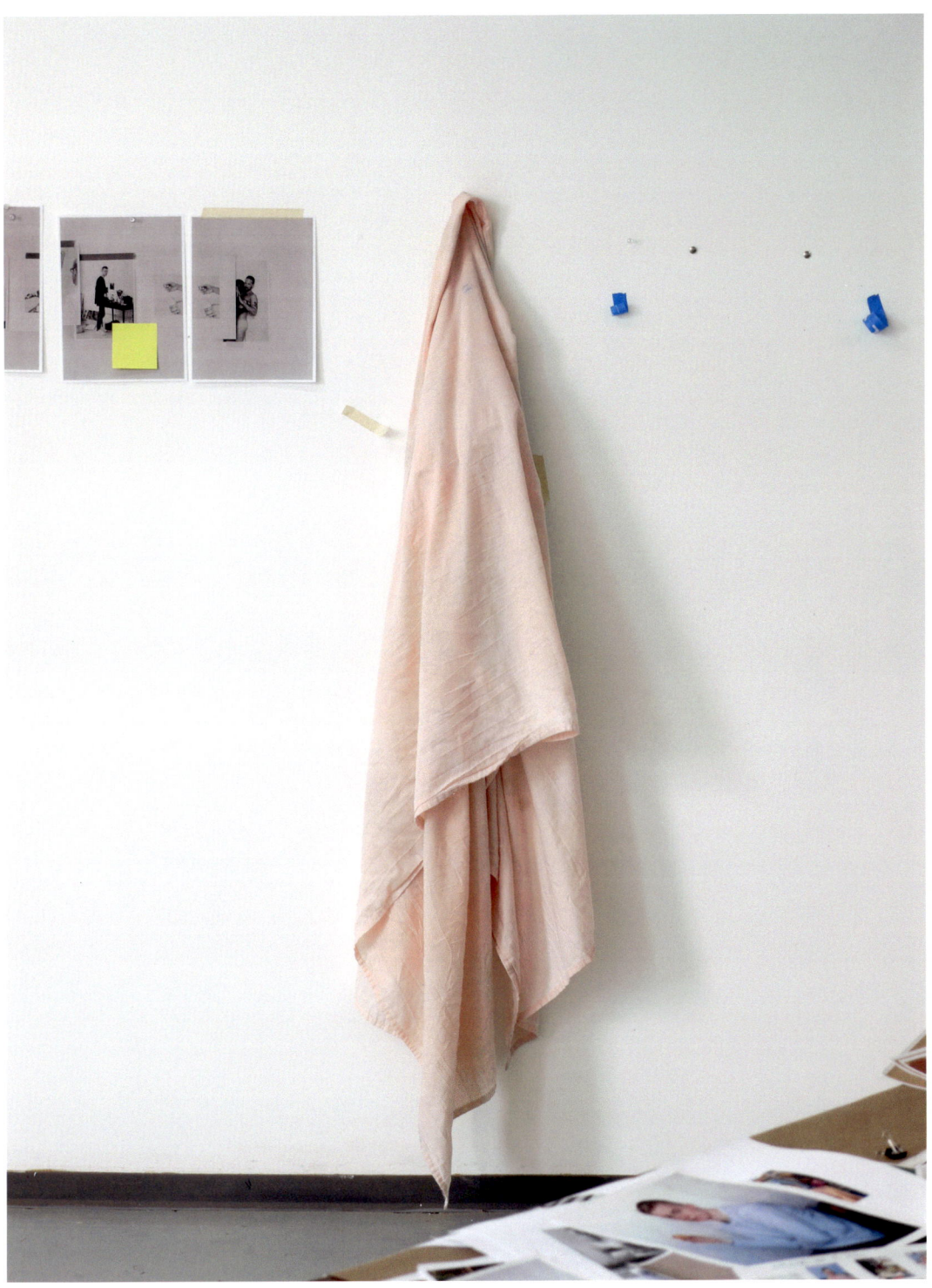

Studio, March 12, 2014

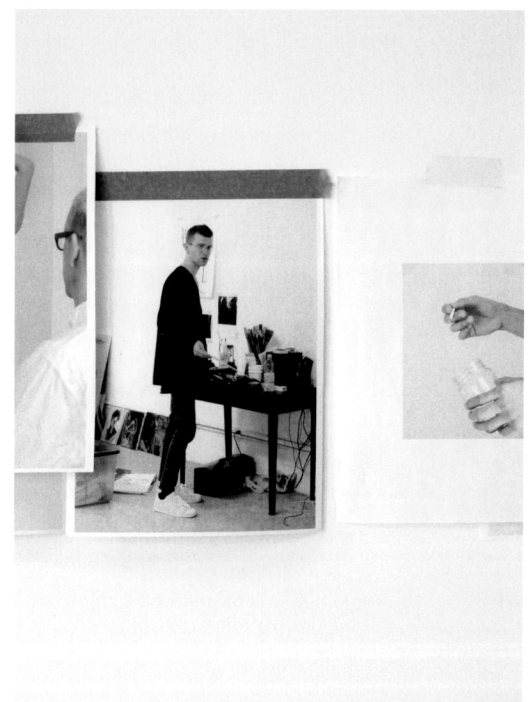 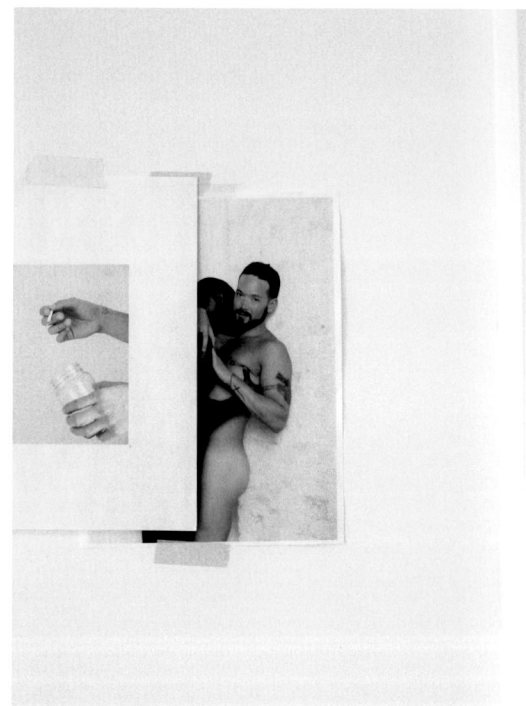

Studio, March 2 (part 1), 2014

Studio, March 2 (part 2), 2014

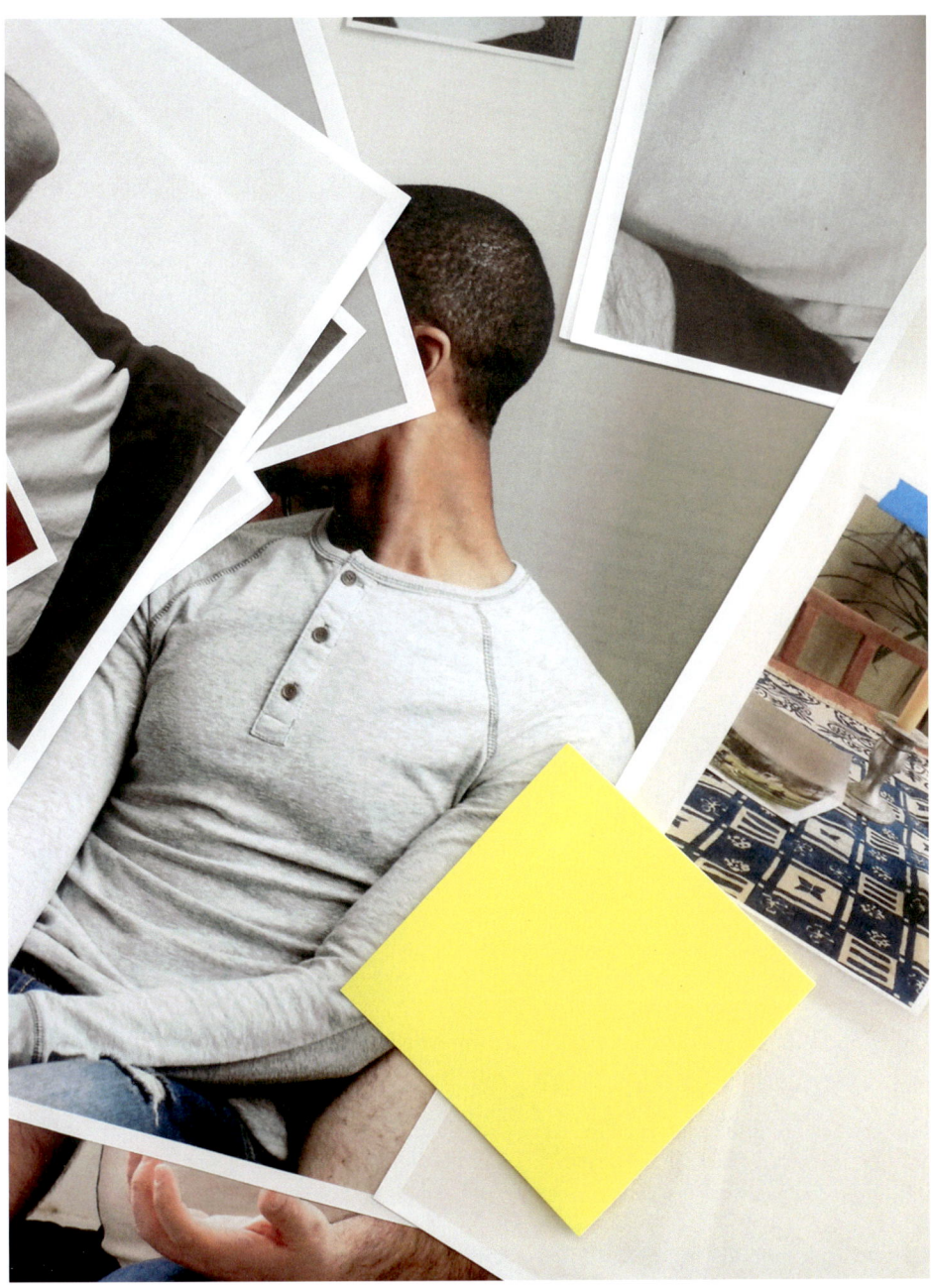

Desktop, April 2, 2014

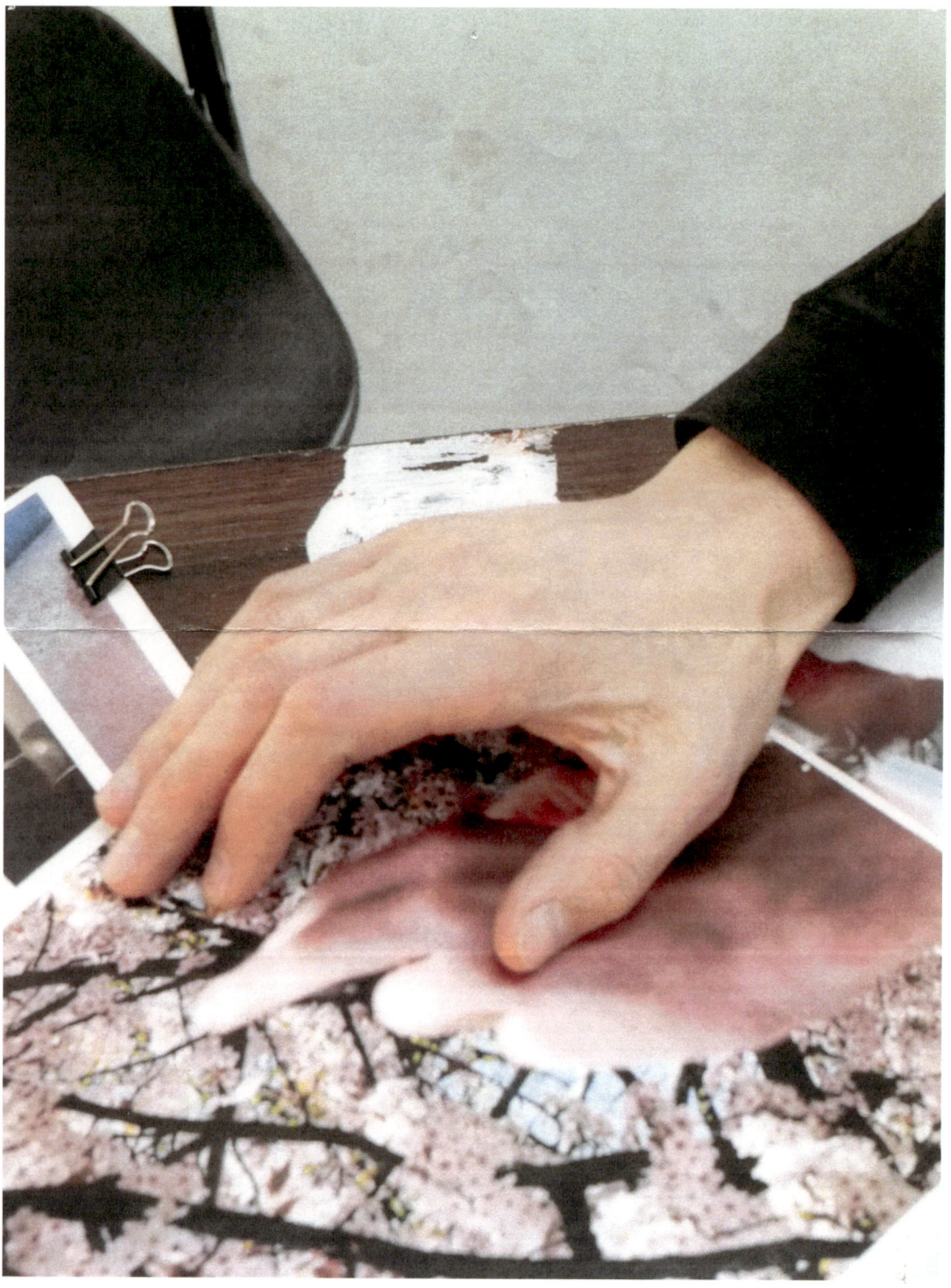

Robert, March 24, 2014

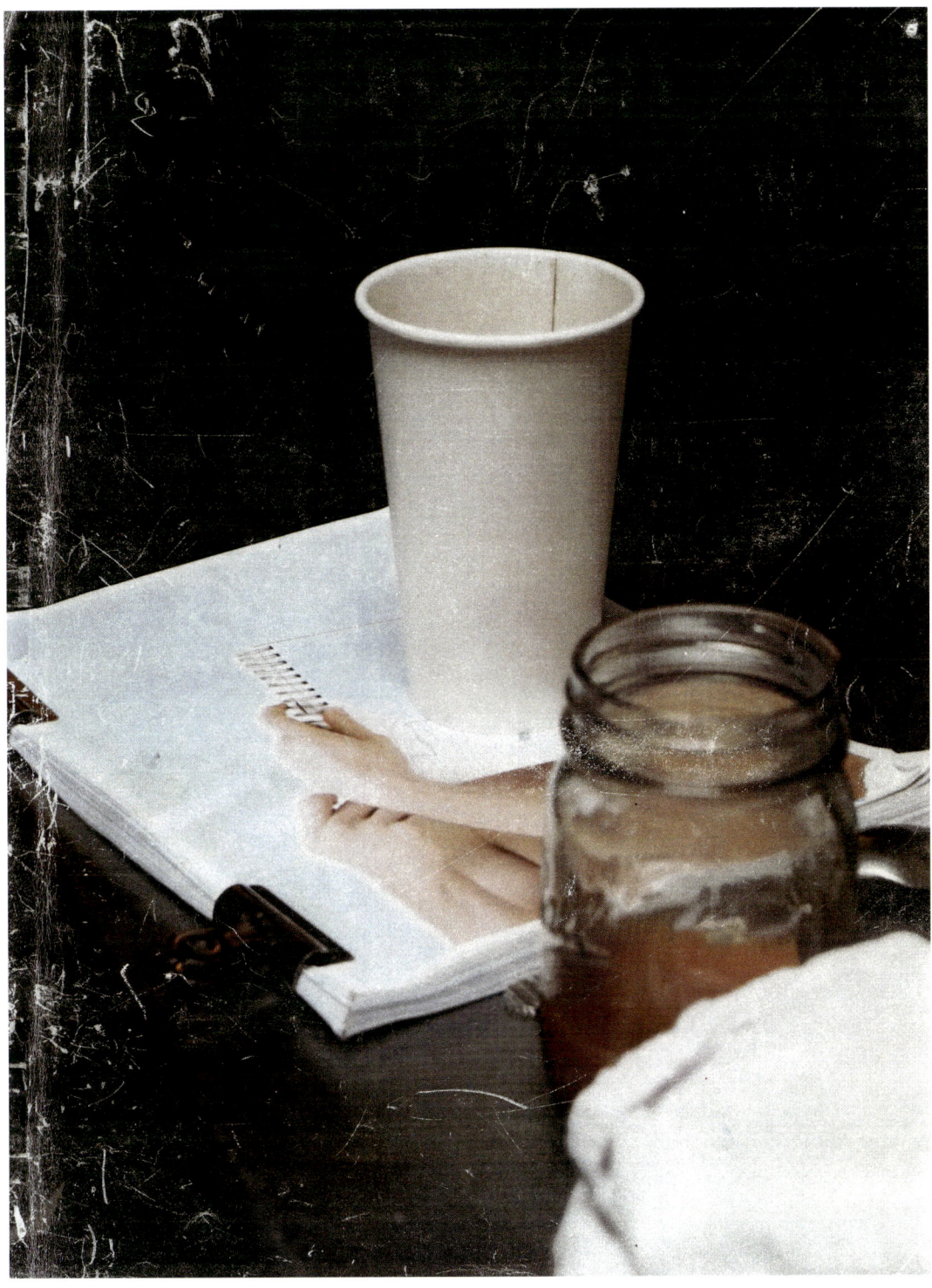

Kitchen, Brooklyn, March 3, 2013–15

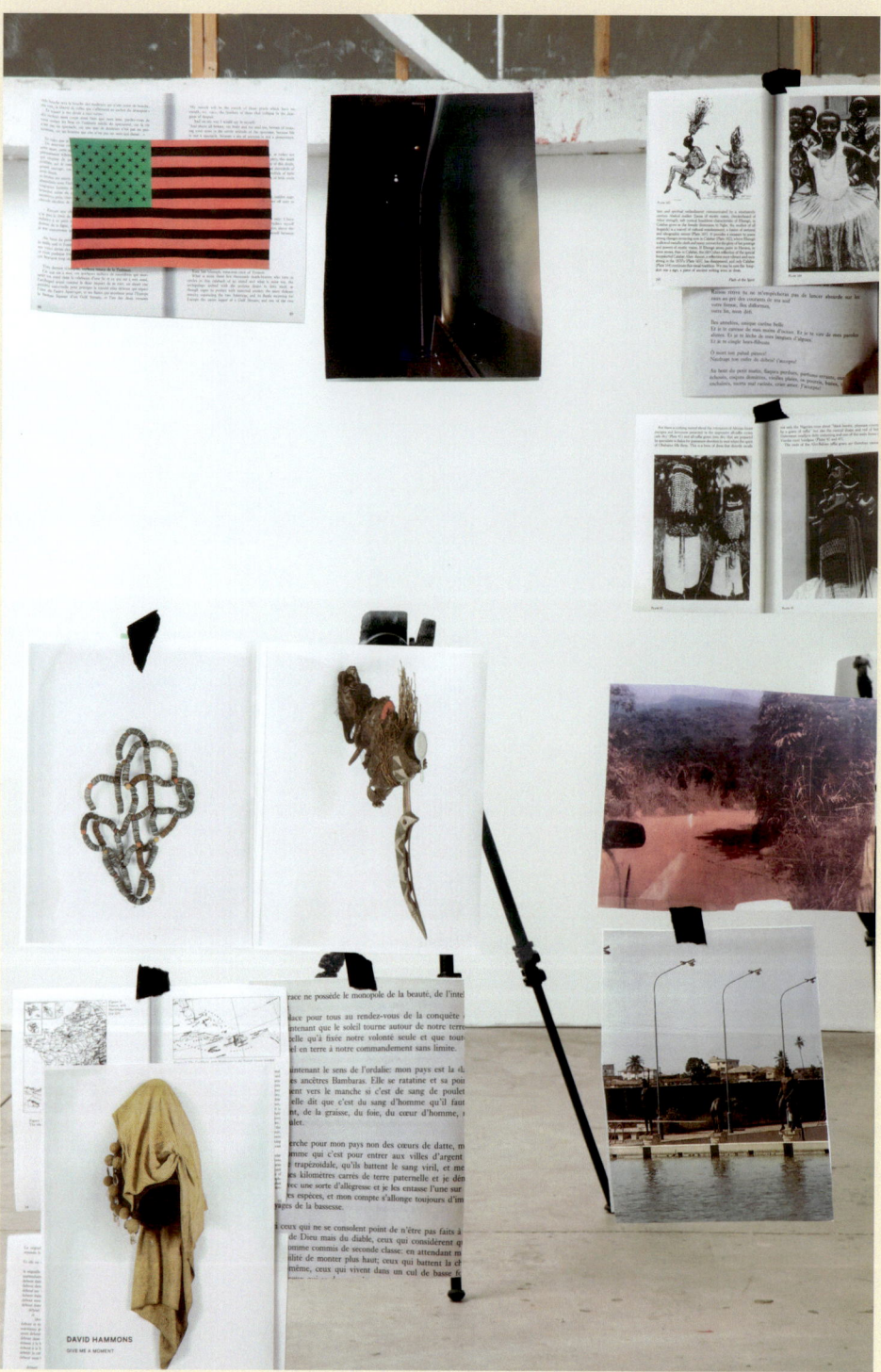

Mirror Study for Grace (0X5A2020), 2017

Fingertips on the mirror accumulating magic, sweat, and dust. That is what I remember from my first visit to Paul's studio in East Los Angeles. The ground was a black velvet, suggestively draped and secured by a black metal photographic stand. The contrast between romanticism (the drapery and tender nudes that adorned the walls) and pragmatic realism (the tools of production) felt so refined. The space felt comfortably familiar, I realized, because I had seen glimpses of it through reflections and fragments in Paul's photographs.

The studio is a central foundation of Paul's practice. Grounded in an understanding of the complexity of representation, Paul's work connects deeply with the history of studio portraiture. In his space, history was ever-present and in flux—the traces of expression imprinted on the mirror, the neat and imaginative arrangements of reference material and his printed works, records of the past available for future works. His photographs appeared transcendently in different iterations throughout the space, organized in ordered grids on the walls, or exploded at scale, collaged and rephotographed in the mirror, or stacked in piles and archived in artists books. I was impressed by the structures Paul had created for himself, that allowed for his genius to flow so effortlessly.

The present felt abundant with potential. Paul's exploration of time felt majestic in its rejection of chronology. His conscious agility in working through parallel temporalities left space for the present to be captured, reframed, and reimagined. This was a real-time recording of the evolution of his development, enhanced because it was so traceable, where each fragment of an image could be sourced to its origin through his meticulous archiving process. His compositions blurred hierarchies of knowledge and the formality of space, creating complex yet harmonious constellations, studies of beauty, dignity, and fragility. I could see how the systems Paul had created supported the richness and depth of his exploration, and most importantly, how they allowed him to be free.

It made sense when Paul explained that he had worked as an archivist for several seminal black artists. The idea of lineage is traced in the soul of the work. I recall Hilton Als describing Paul as a child of James Baldwin at Als's Baldwin show at The Artist's Institute. Similarly, his work belongs to the lineage of Rotimi Fani-Kayode in its precise vocabulary, distinctive perspective, and unfaltering presence. Paul is guided by a deep knowledge of what has come before, the past that perhaps shapes the potential of the present moment—an ancestral world connected to a different sense of time, or timelessness.

Plates
Studies

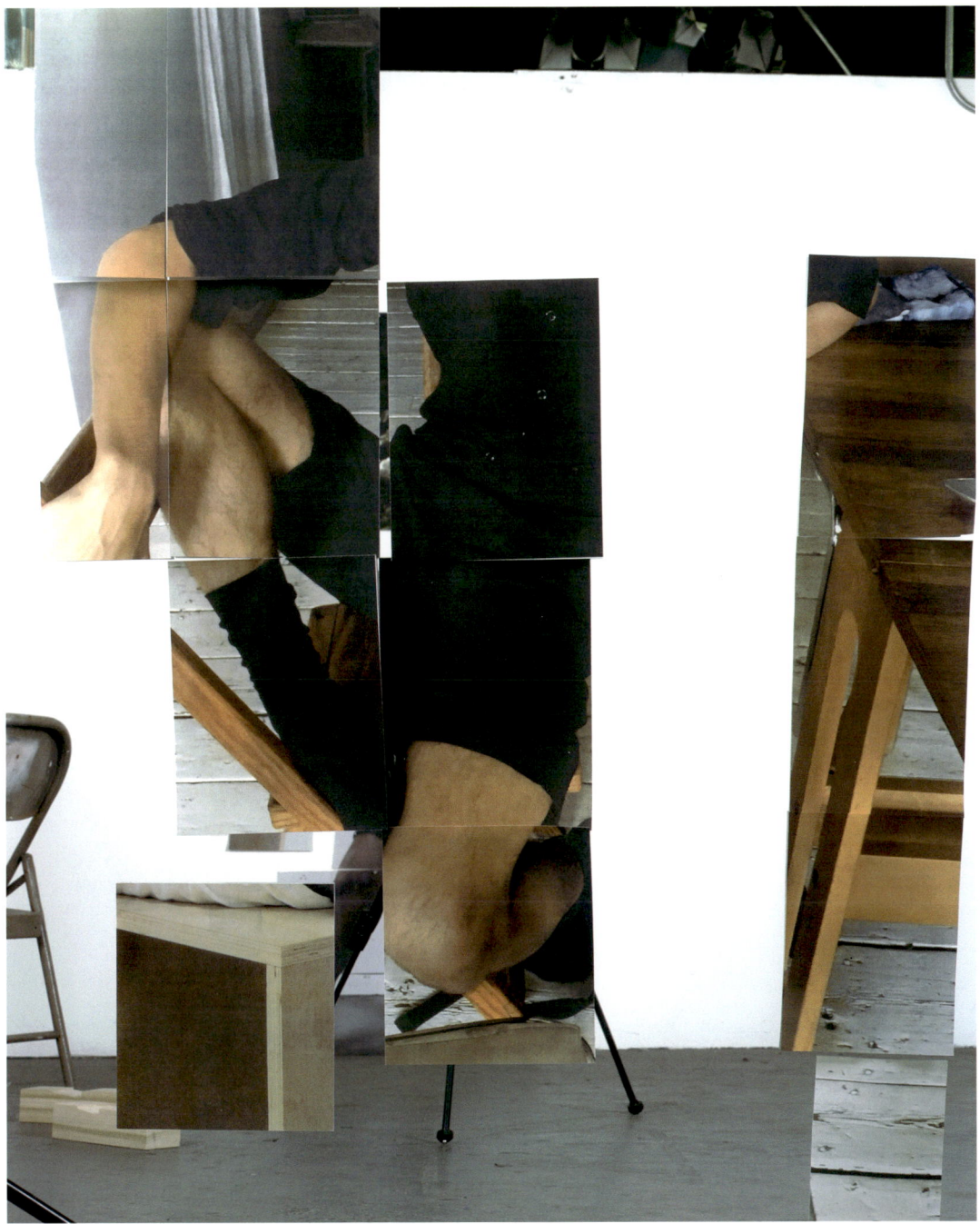

Study for T.H. with Two Figures (2005), 2015

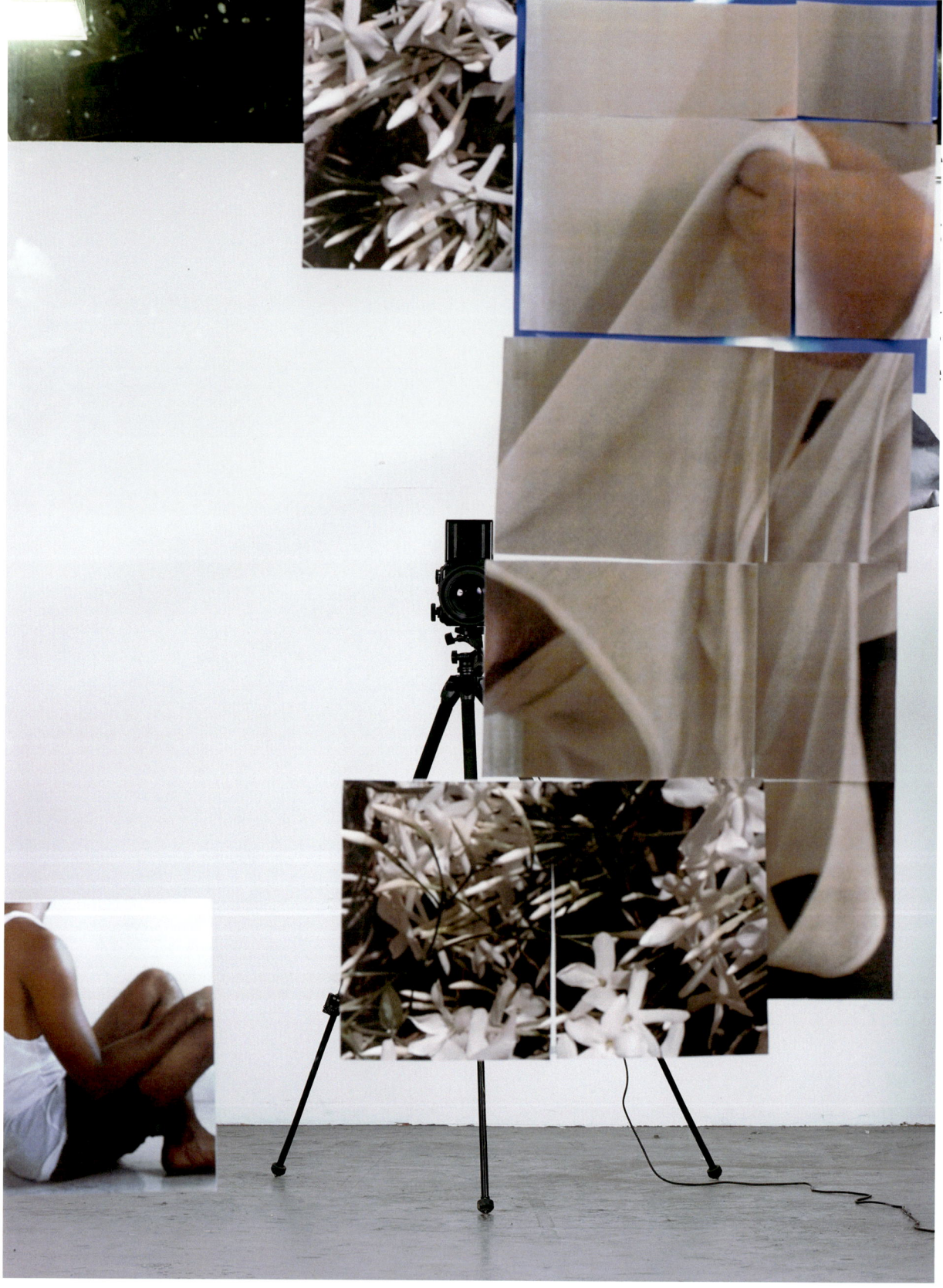

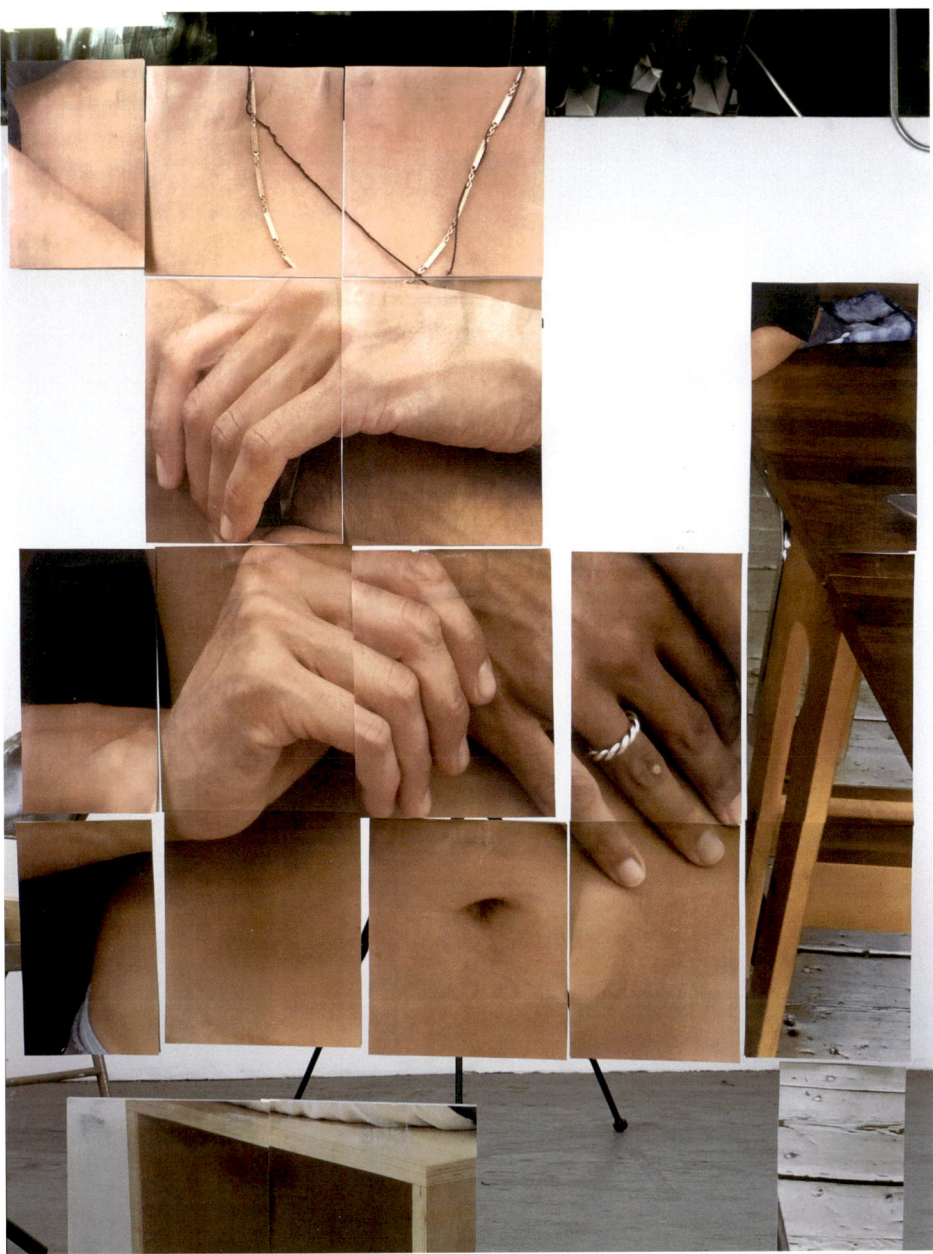

Five Figures (3002), 2016 *Study for friendship, D.C.S. and F.C. (2106)*, 2015

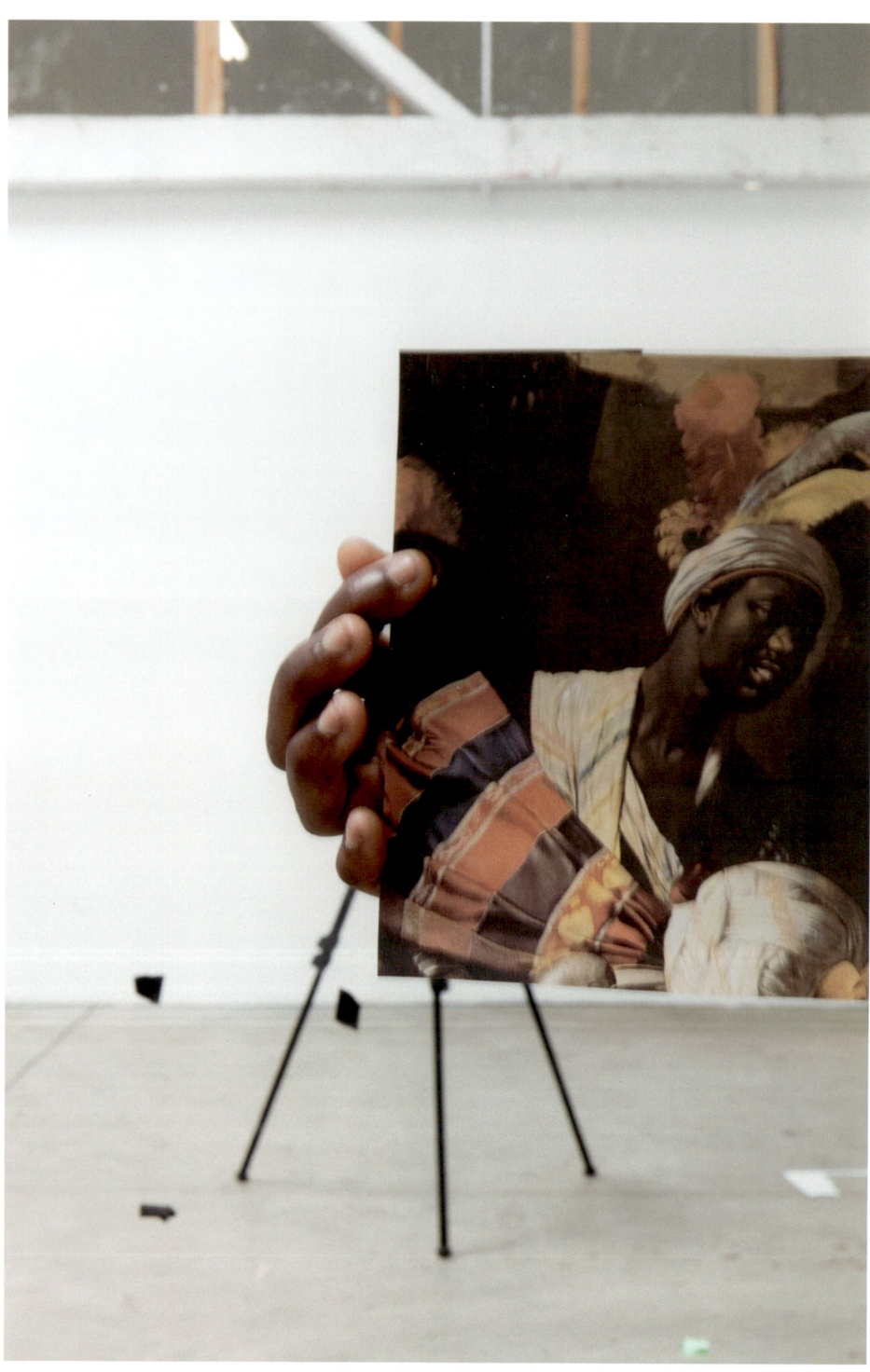

Mirror Study for Grace (0X5A2066), 2017

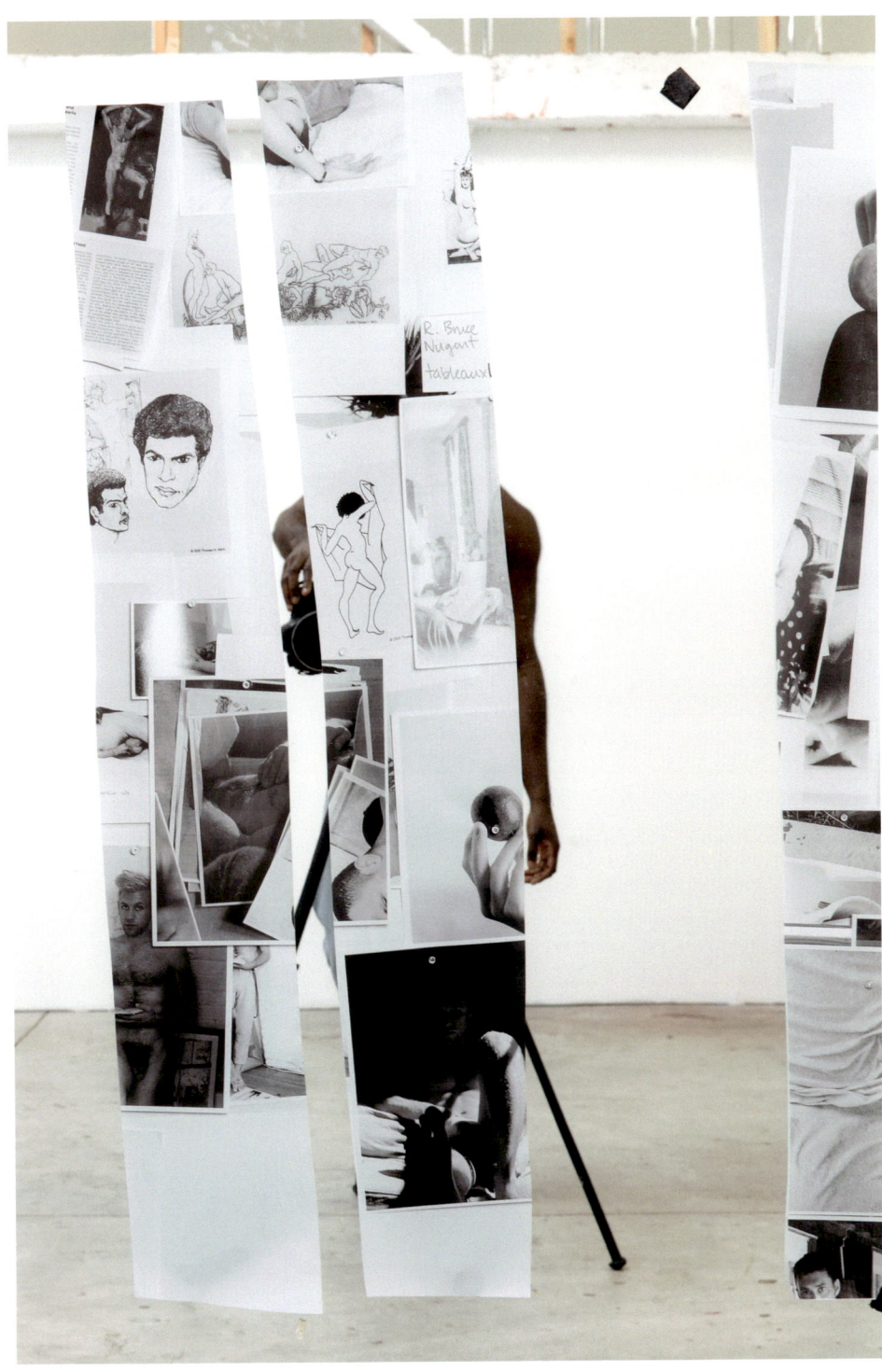

Studio (0X5A0173), 2017

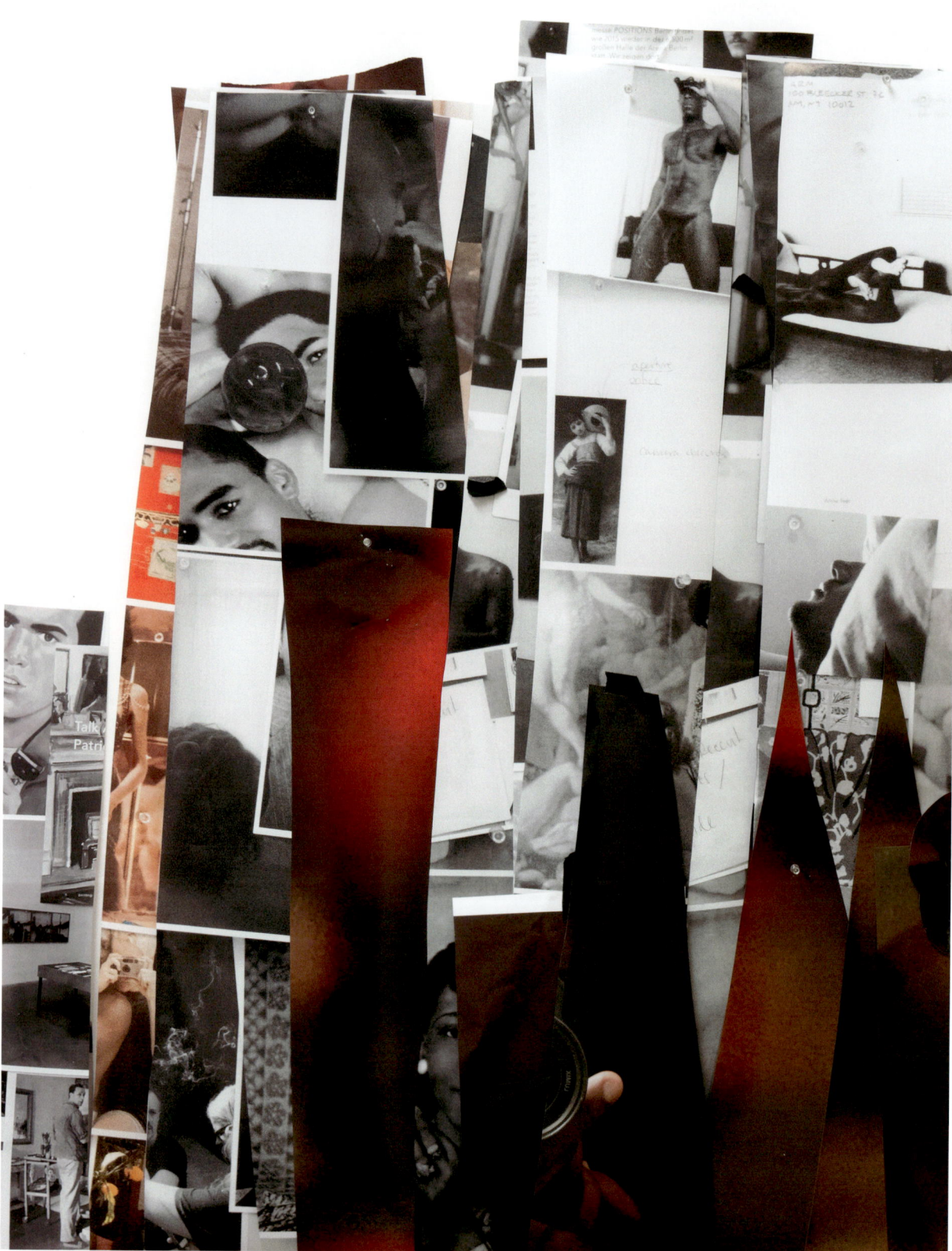

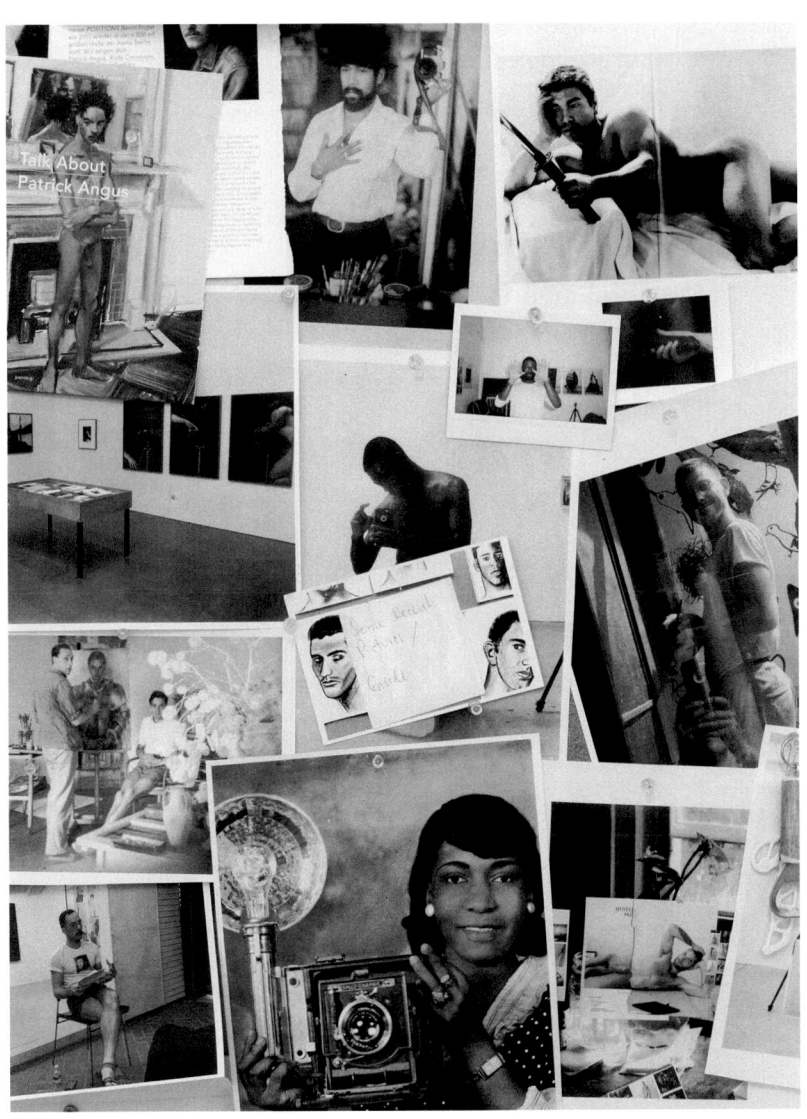

Studio Wall (_1000021), 2018

Studio (_2150762), 2017

Much rests on the singular, when there is no good reason for it. Into Paul Mpagi Sepuya's fragments of documents of reflections of collaborations made into compositions, one might project a fantasy of a more ethical representation, an image of a better mode of democracy, a parliament of parts that is other-reflexive.

Paul used to take pictures of cute guys. These documented his homosociality: the members of his queer mini-culture made seamless and framed. These were beautiful and desire-affirming photographs. They offered clarity and wholeness to bodies that had been obscured and misconstrued in an at-large regime of visuality. They may have been too pretty for some purposes, although perfect for others.

Nearly a decade ago, while I was in grad school, I organized a group show as a way to think in the present about a premise in my writing about the past. Around the work of Nina Simone, I had imagined an idea of "quadruple consciousness" as a multiplication of Du Bois's famous formulation, offering a multiple positionality, a way to keep moving, and a resistance to the categorical thrust of the human/nonhuman dyad, a way to be extra. For this exhibition Paul offered a diptych: an image of a handsome young man whose appearance and attire suggested Arab situations, and a photo of a photo on top of another photo that included a shot of Simone wearing pharaonic Egyptiana. Many distances made near.

Being around Paul is to be enlisted in his photographic sociality. There is realism in his image world, despite its deliberate and radical occlusions and reframing. The first time I saw myself in Paul's work was in a collage that included a shot of the back of my head while I was seated at a piano. He had participated in a performance Alexandro Segade and I had coordinated, and in that process some images were absorbed into his camera: a real reciprocity between gays, a documentation of lives, a constructed scenario, and time-based action. The photo reverses portrait orientation, centering not on the face I present, which speaks and expresses, which is the subject of recognition, but gives a view from behind, a pianist's pose, and a proximity afforded to those who have experienced me as a bottom.

There is sex around and within these images, a particularly sustaining form of queer sociality.

Not long ago, I wanted a new headshot for my faculty profile page. I had noticed a couple such photos that curators at the Studio Museum in Harlem had procured from Paul's camera following his residency there. In both, the curators seemed so assured with their arms crossed in front of them; I wanted that too.

I went to Paul's studio in LA and got the shot, and offered to pose for his work in exchange. A veteran performance artist, I was quick to undress. I worked with Paul in arrangements that are familiar to his recent work. We sat before a smudged mirror with a camera in between, some black velvet curtains marking out a dark dimensional space. He put me in positions with him and his camera, so that parts of each of us appeared to be in each reflected image.

This work that depicts dis-unified body parts in the act of image-making goes much deeper than the surface on which a particular living social sphere interacts. In much of the leading black philosophy that informs my work, from the Fred Moten-esque form of black study, to the scholars working in the black feminist wakes of Hortense Spillers and Sylvia Wynter, such as in the radical reinventions of the archive Saidiya Hartman produces, and even in the Afro-pessimism of Frank B. Wilderson and Jared Sexton my students find so energizing, the legacy that has produced the autonomous individual is shown to be a brutally violent legacy of misdirection. Philosophically, it just doesn't add up. The proposition of being is revised in all of this work, resisting the compulsory forms that support racial capital, colonial adventure, the criminality of the un-citizen-like. A whole range of impossible conditions is signaled in Moten's own titular prompt: *consent not to be a single being.*

I draw so much from many of these thinkers in my own thinking, including new writing that wonders about abstractive forms of democracy that might reorient our decrepit representational apparatuses. How might we account for parts of bodies, bodies in groups, the bodies that live in our bodies?

Now, having sat for Paul, I encounter images of myself in the world that offer a glimpse of this revised representation. In a museum I find my arm. In a gallery, a leg. On Instagram, where someone has visited his studio, my lower half in relation to other fragments, human and nonhuman. With the camera in view, nakedly producing representations, these juxtapositions offer ways of seeing being together: beyond the individual, apart from wholes, short of the beautifully re-represented, in excess of the frame. I feel ready for us to be dismantled in this way.

Plates
Mirror Studies

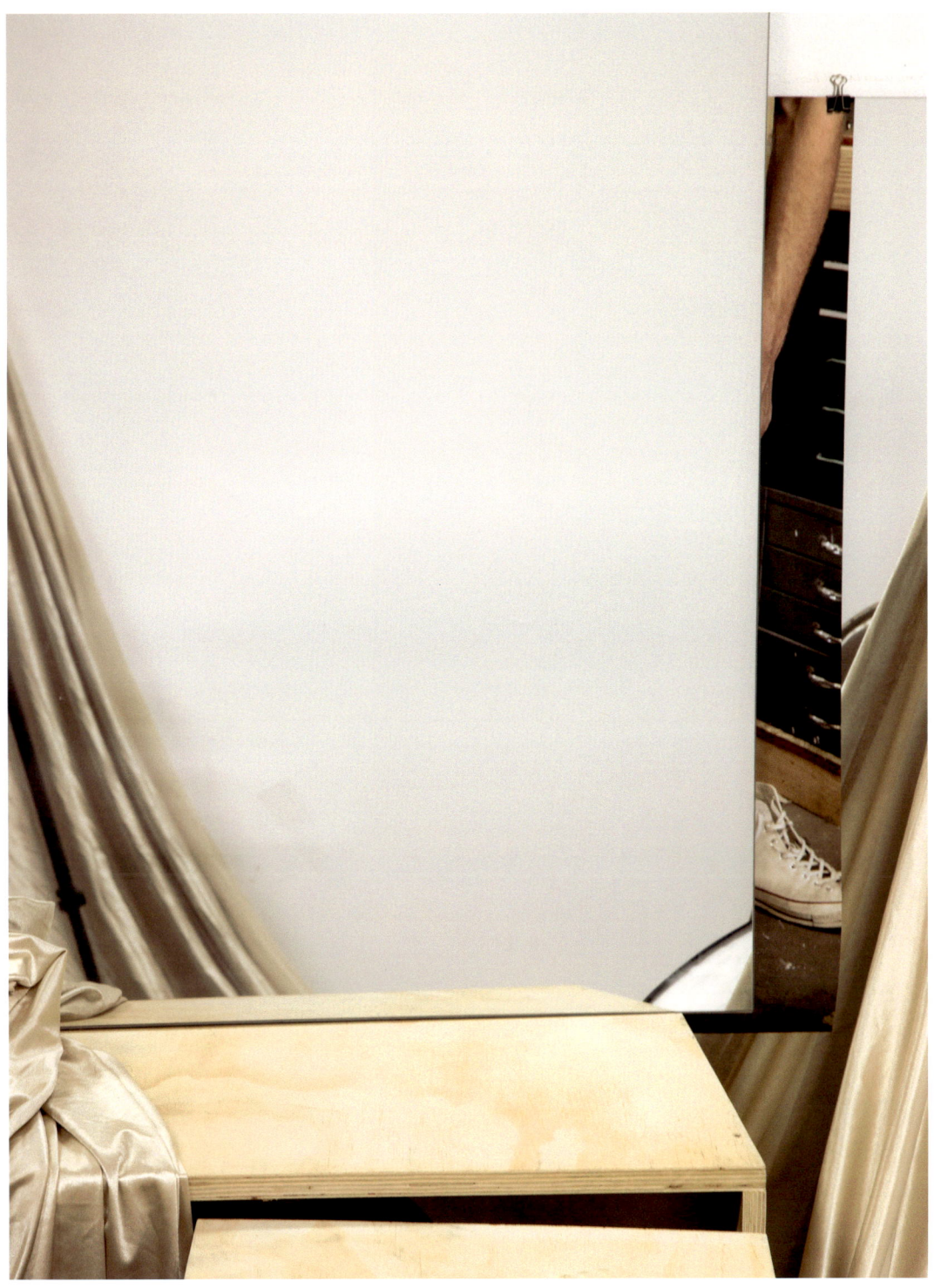

A Ground (File0083), 2015

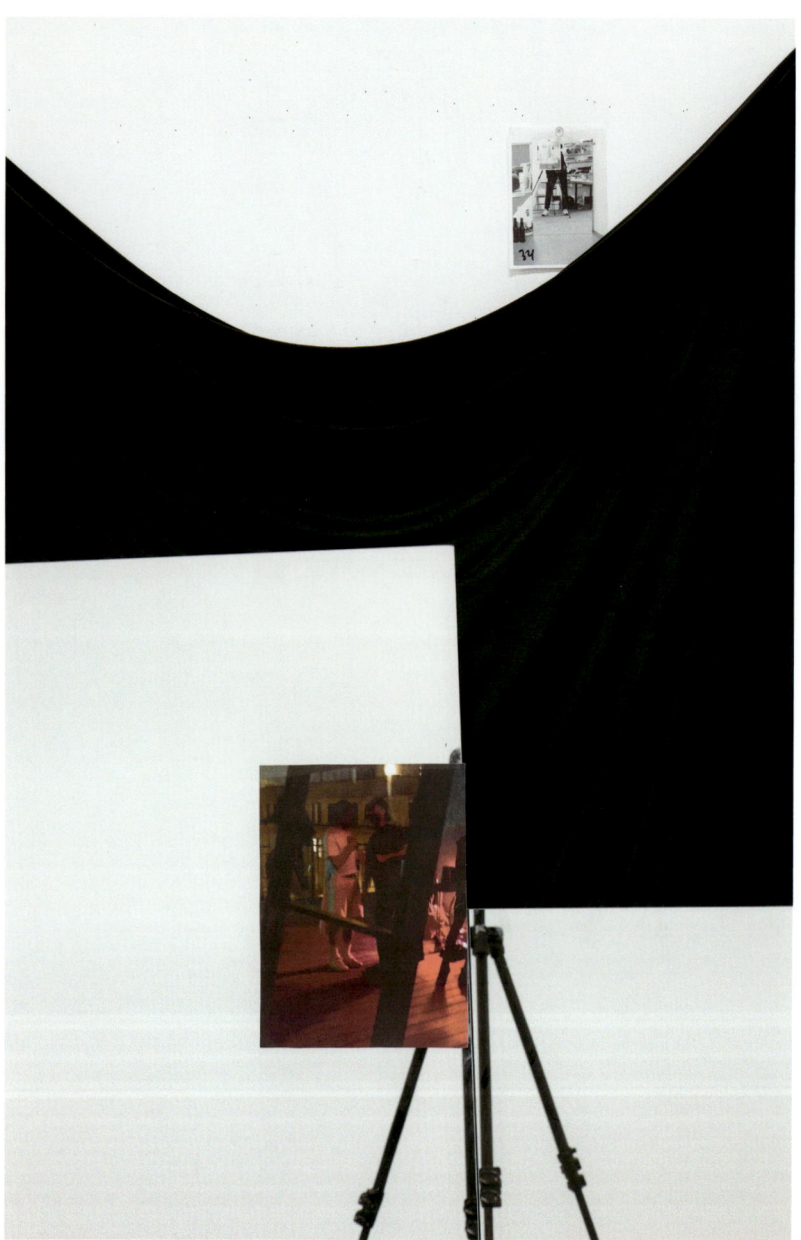

Study (_R2A9181), 2015

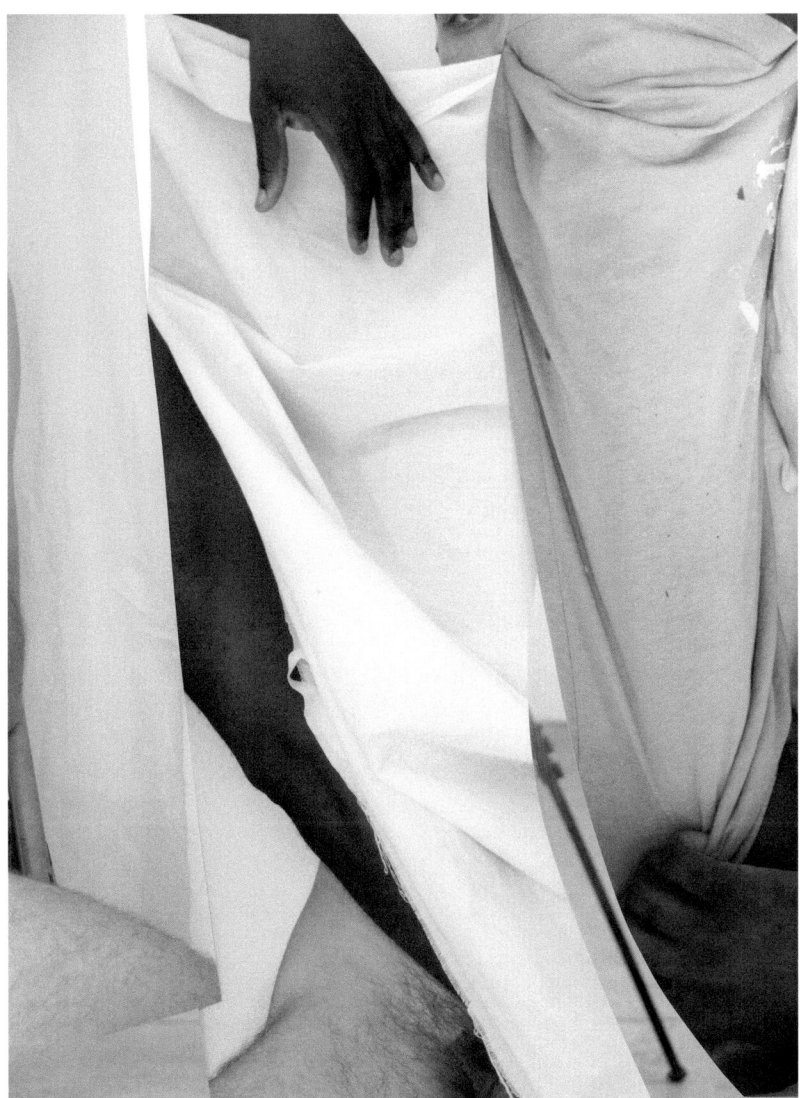

Figure Ground Study (_2000769), 2017

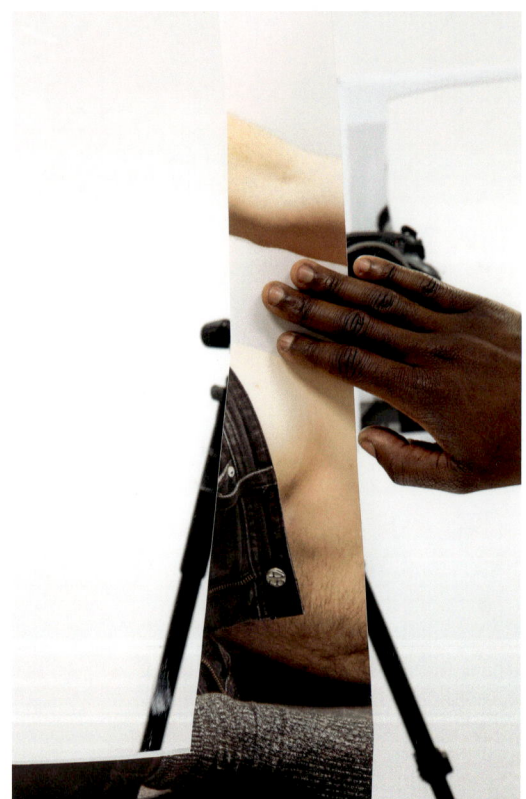

Mirror Study (_Q5A2097), 2016

Mirror Study (4R2A0857), 2016

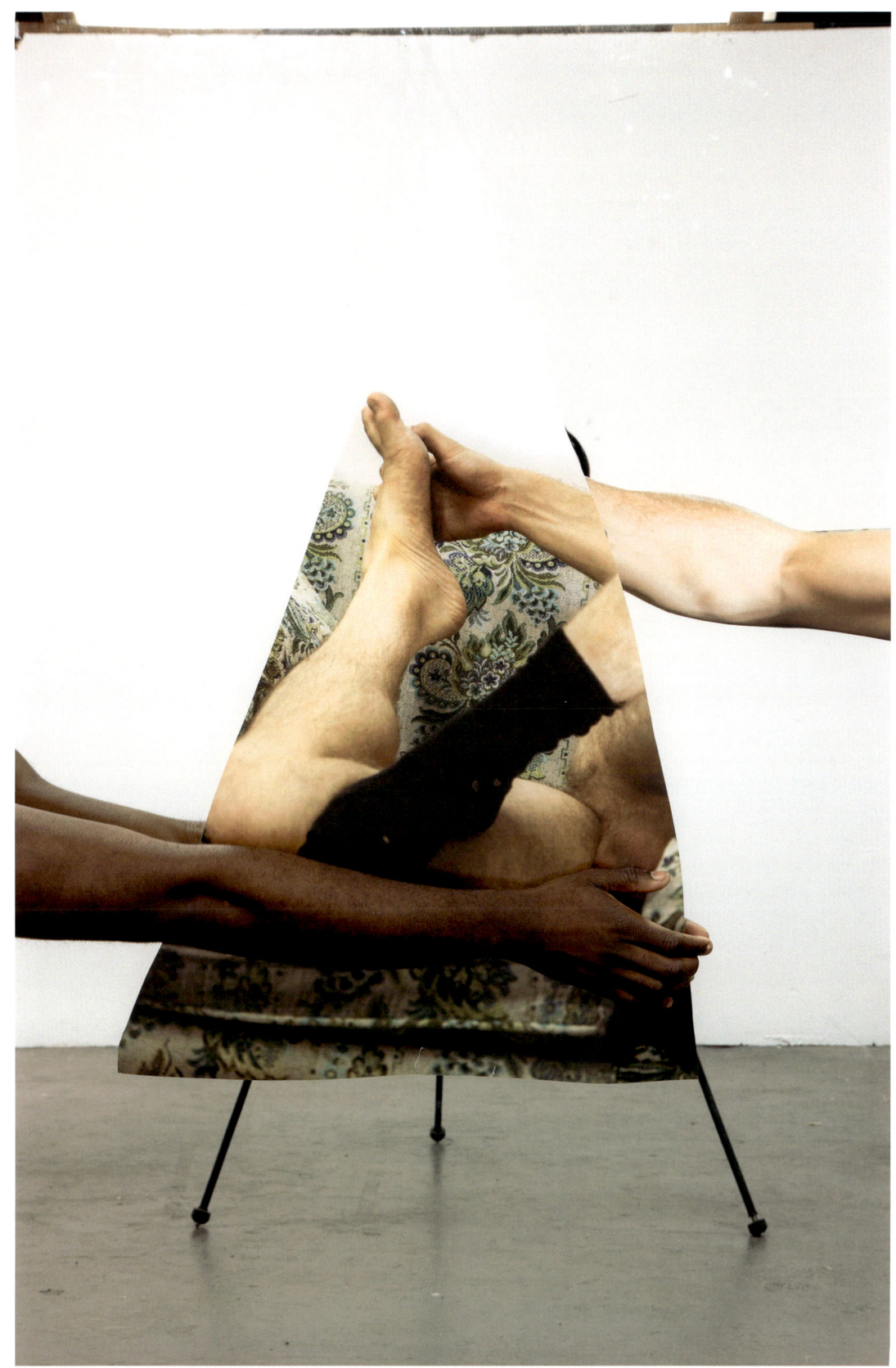

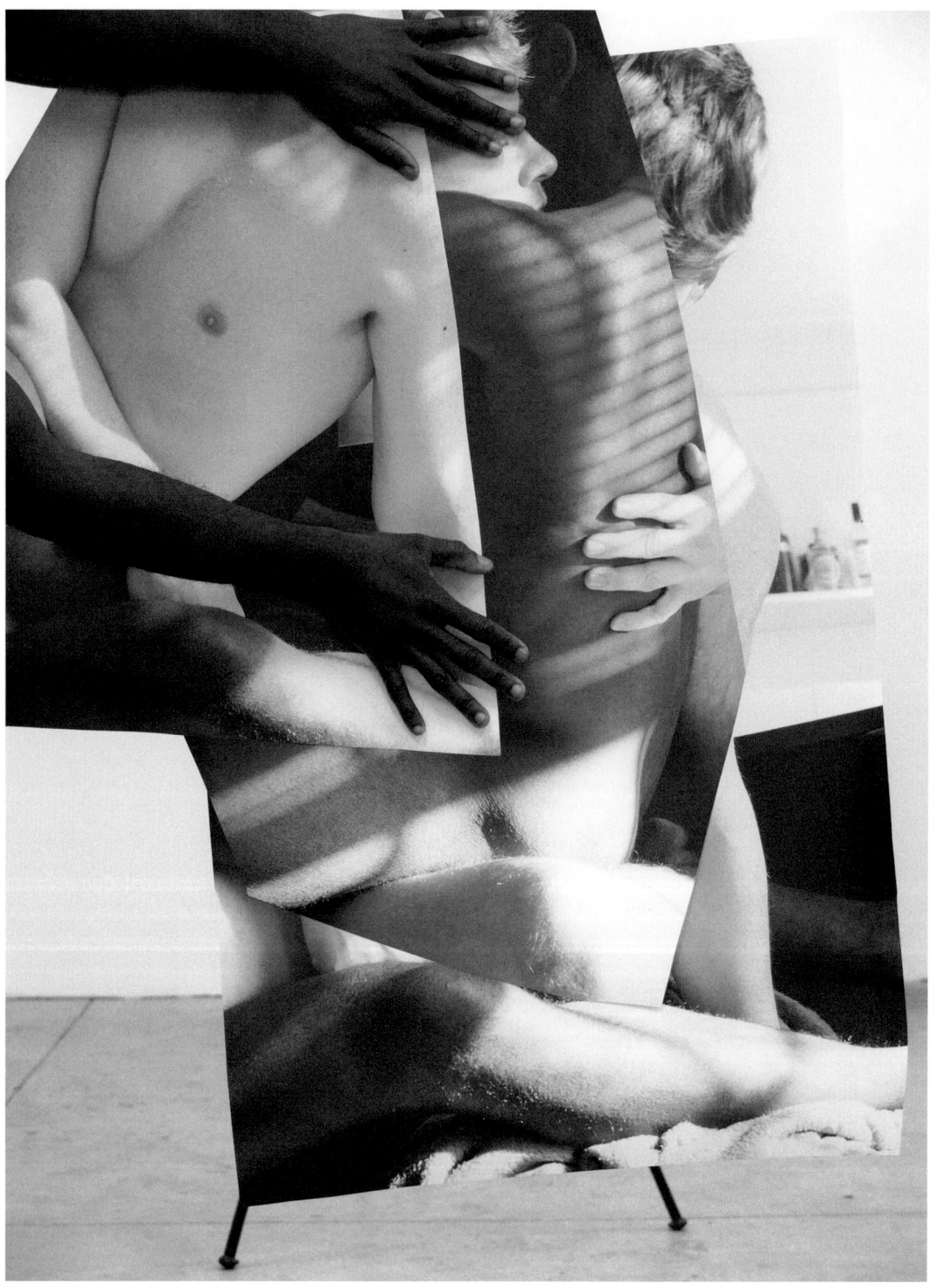

Mirror Study for Joe (_2010980), 2017

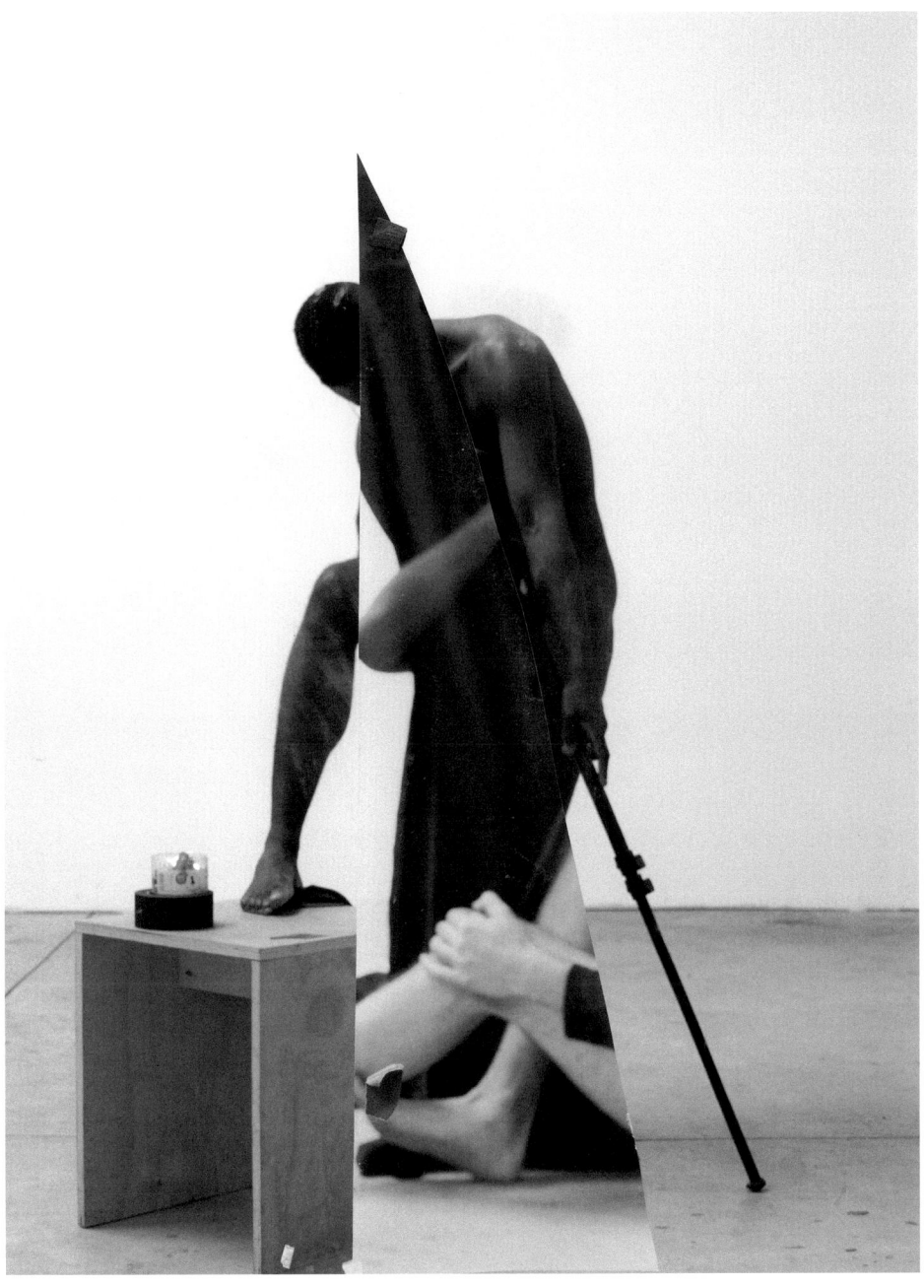

Figure (_2010037), 2017

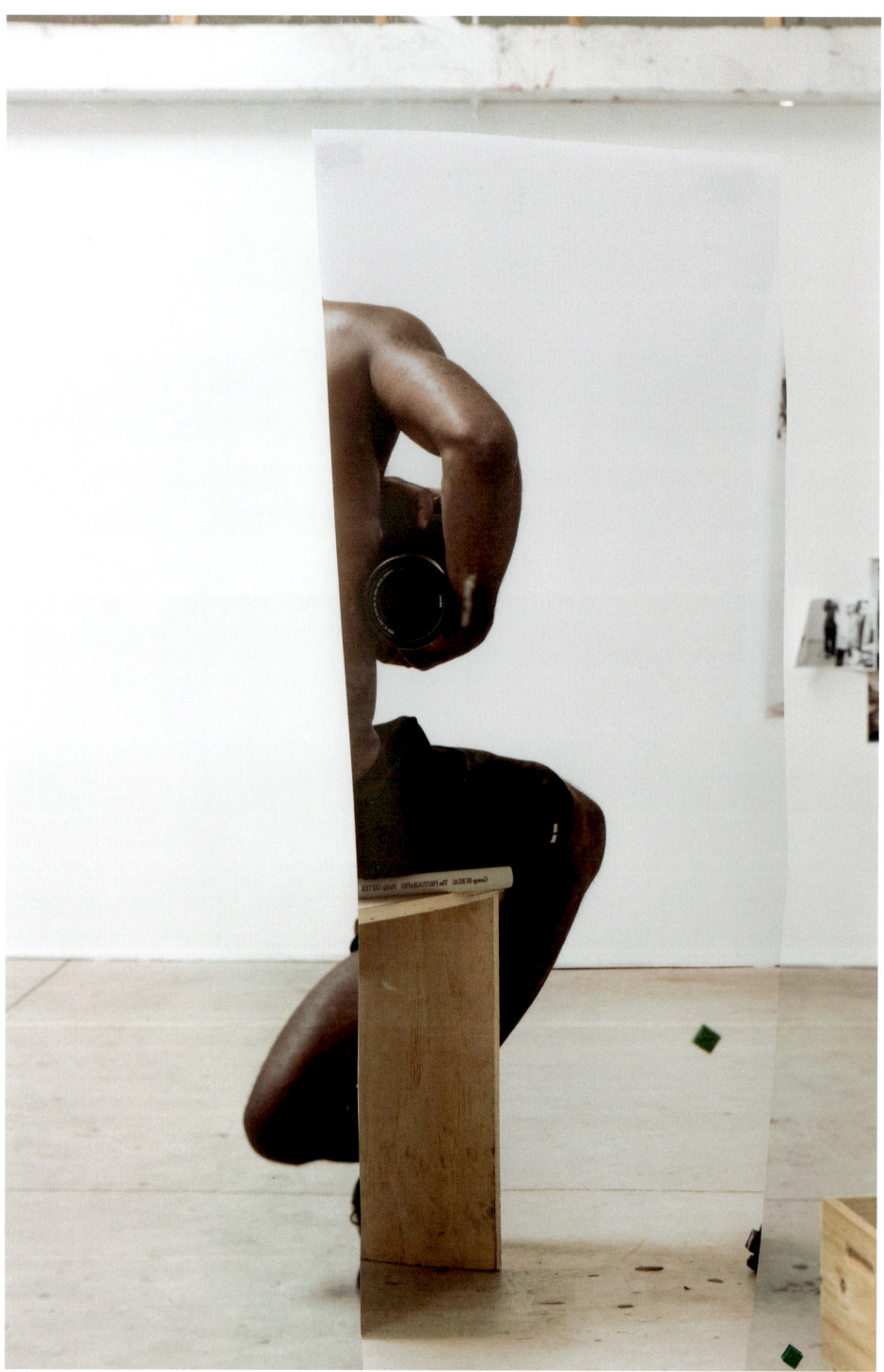

Mirror Study (0X5A1317), 2017

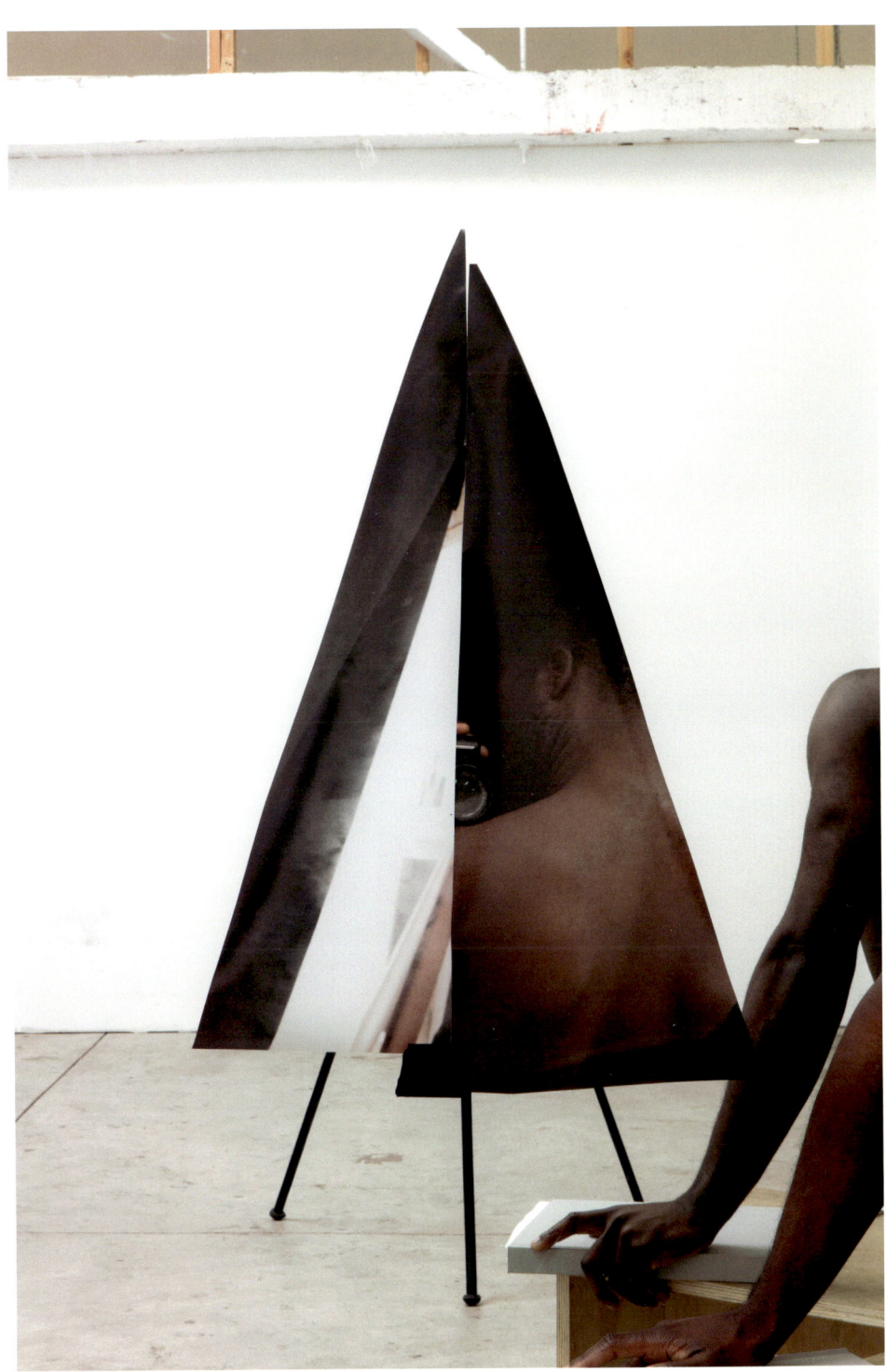

Mirror Study (0X5A7394), 2018

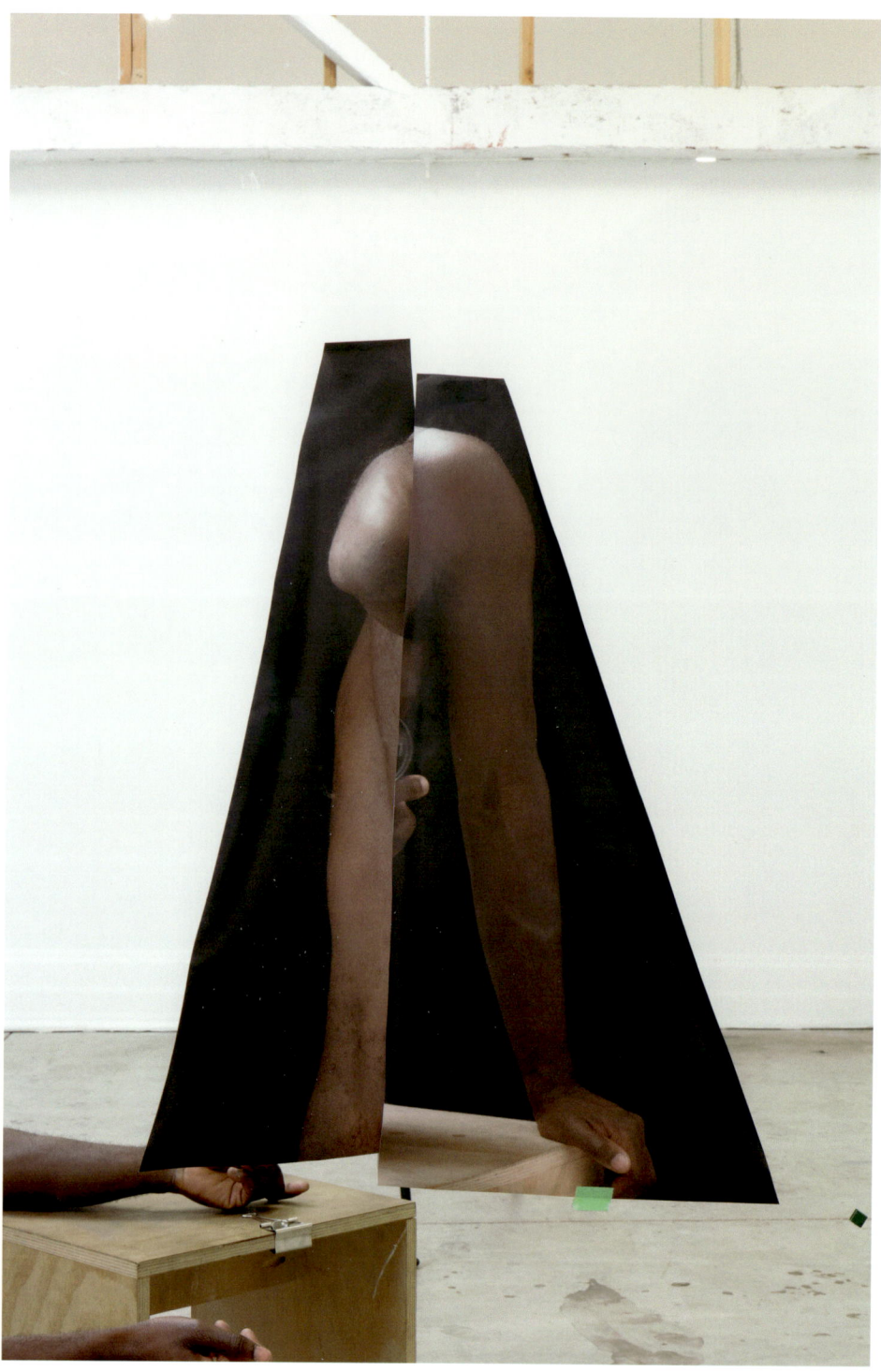

Mirror Study (0X5A7421), 2018

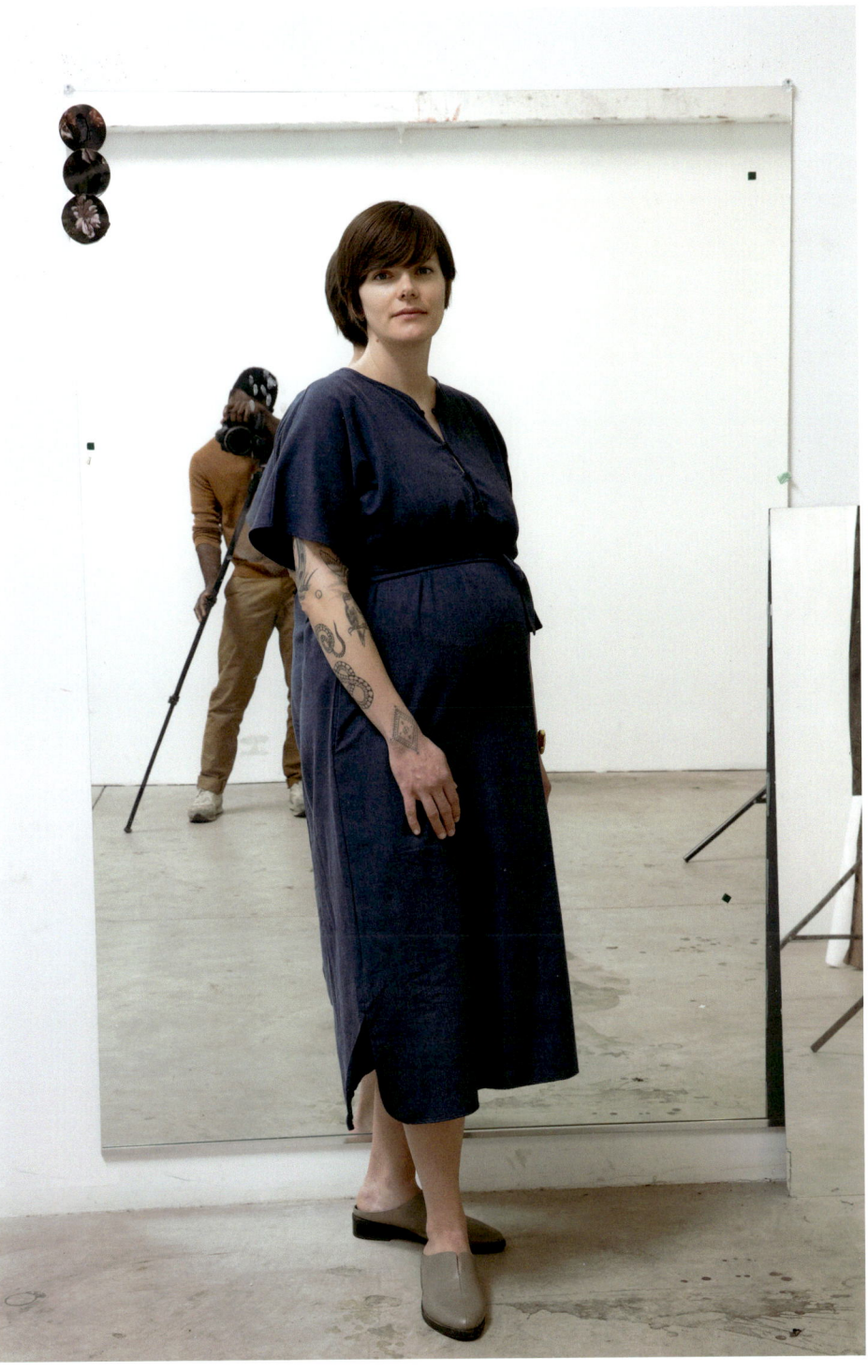

A Portrait (0X5A6109), 2017

Plates
Dark Room

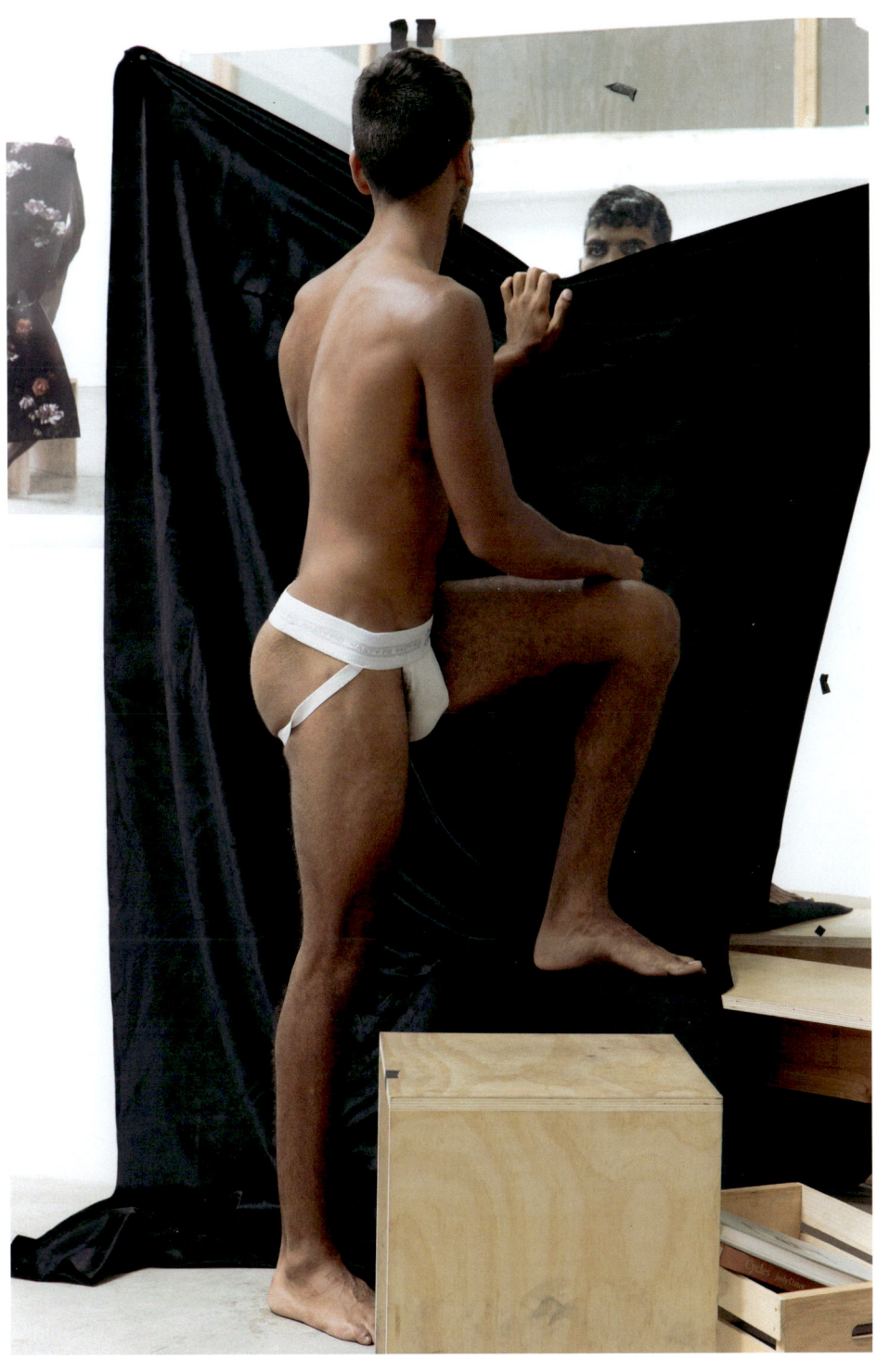

Model Study (0X5A3973), 2017

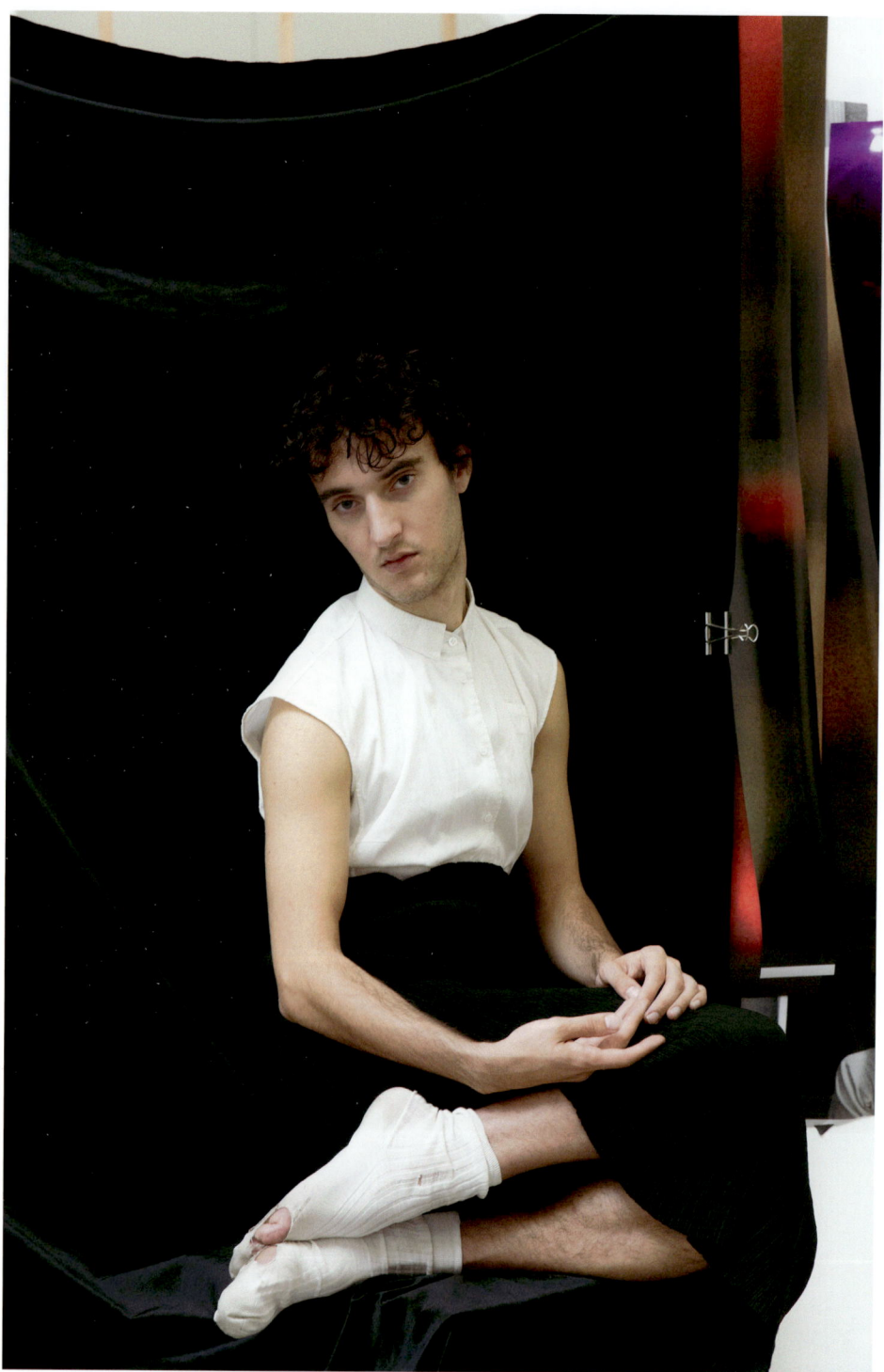

A Portrait (0X5A8325), 2018

Darkroom Mirror Study (_1990750), 2016

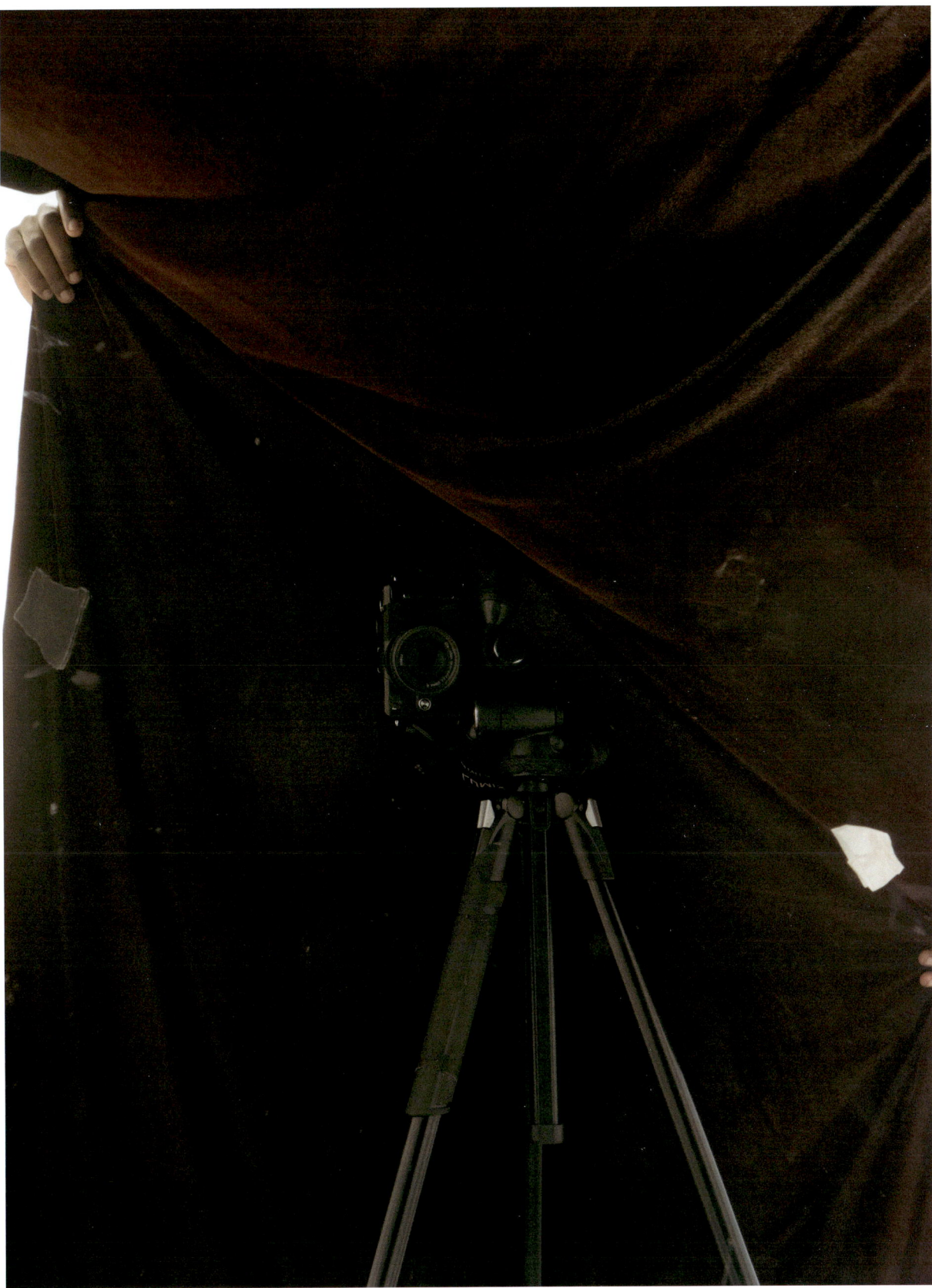

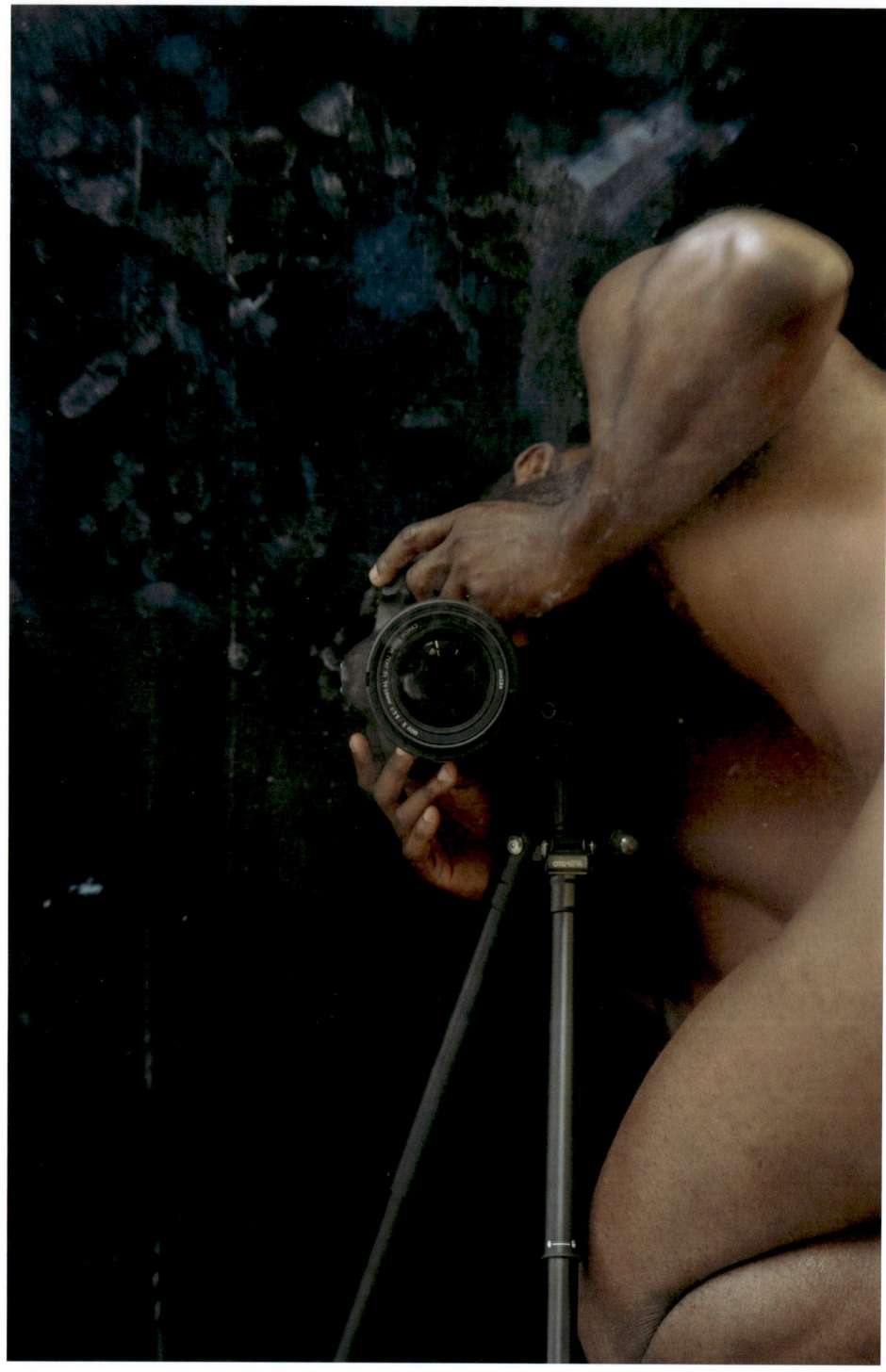

Darkroom Mirror Study (0X5A1531), 2017

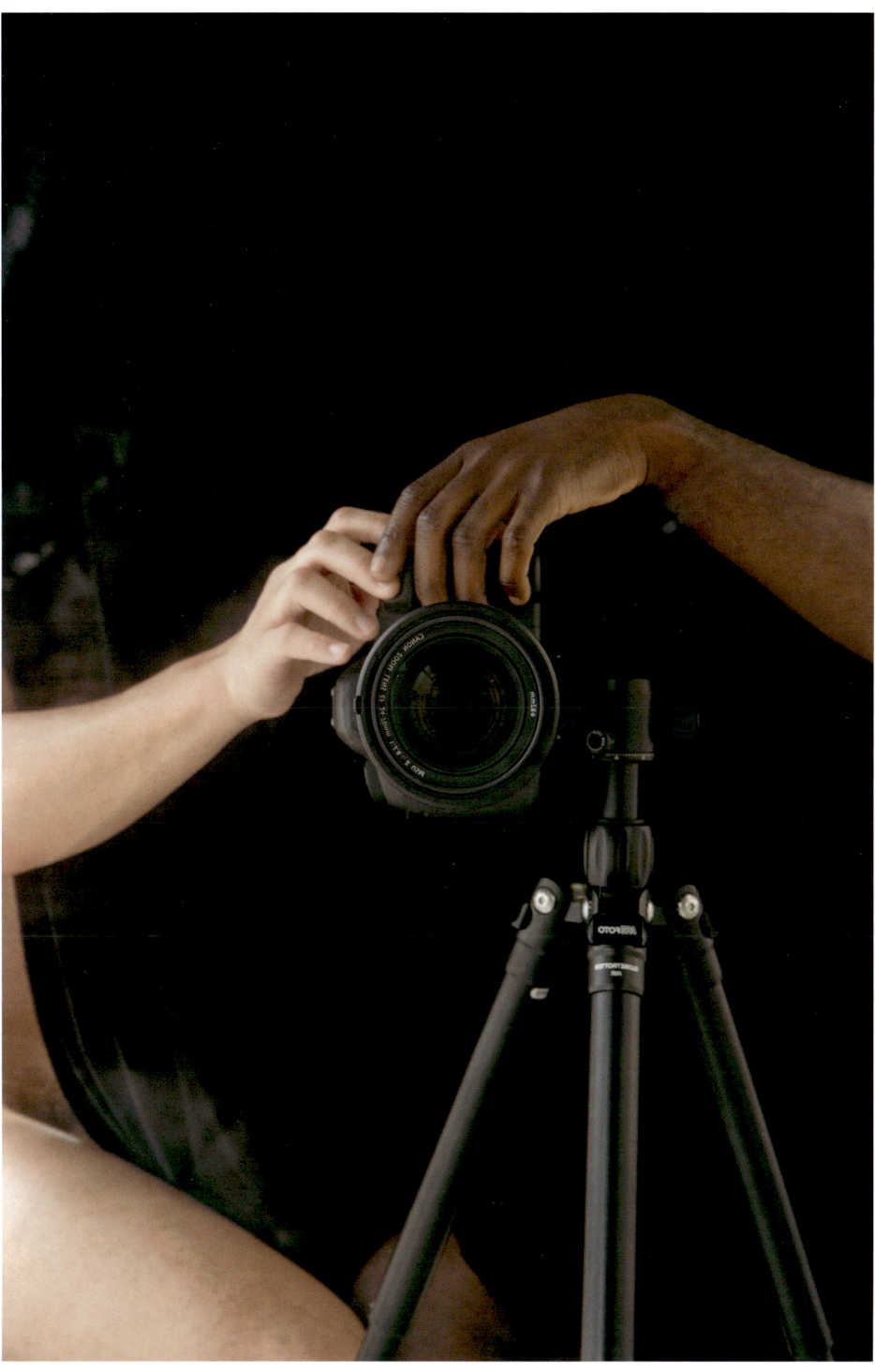

Darkroom Mirror Study (0X5A1812), 2017

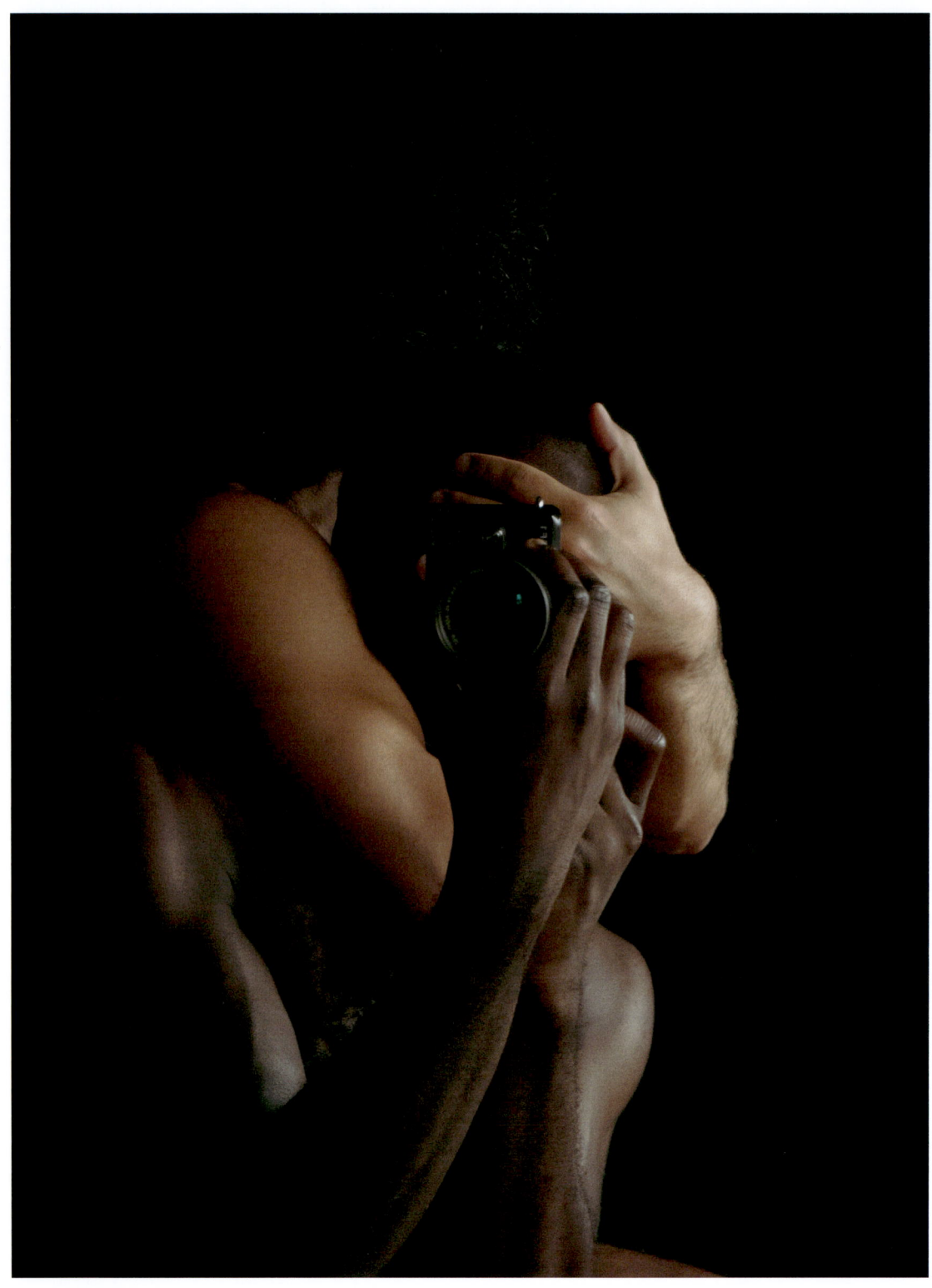

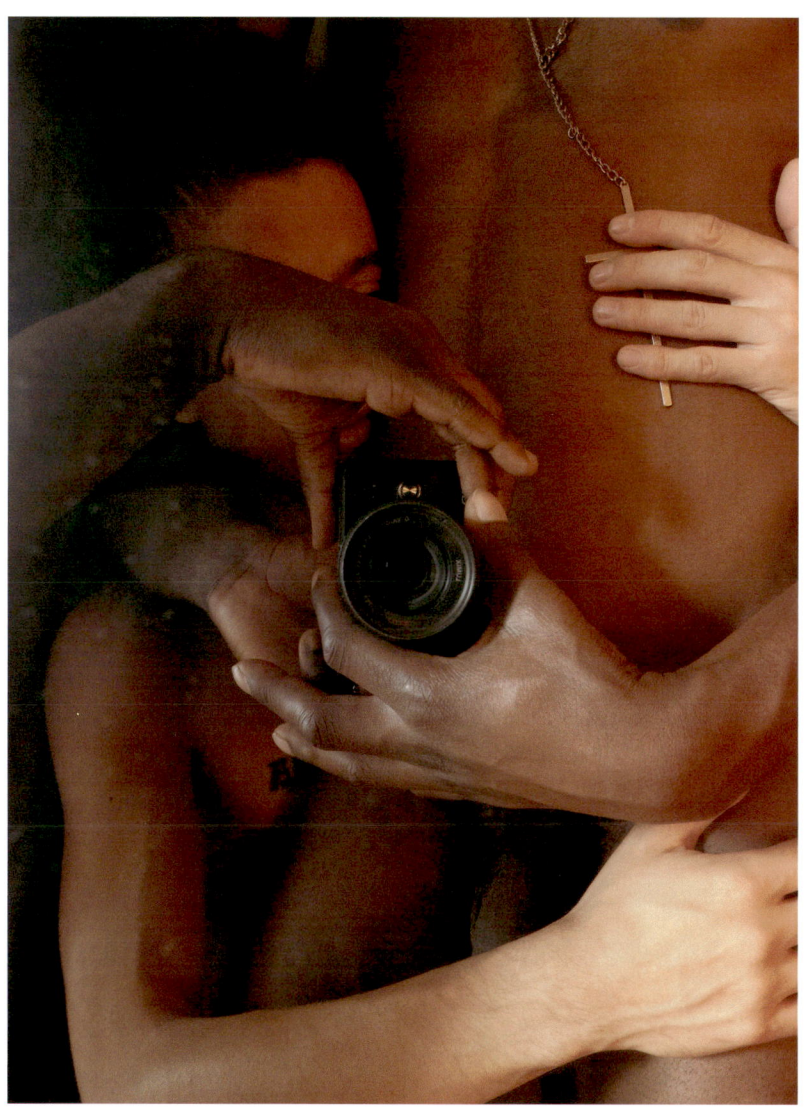

Darkroom Mirror (_2070386), 2017

Darkroom Mirror (_2060999), 2017

Dark Room (0X5A2919), 2017

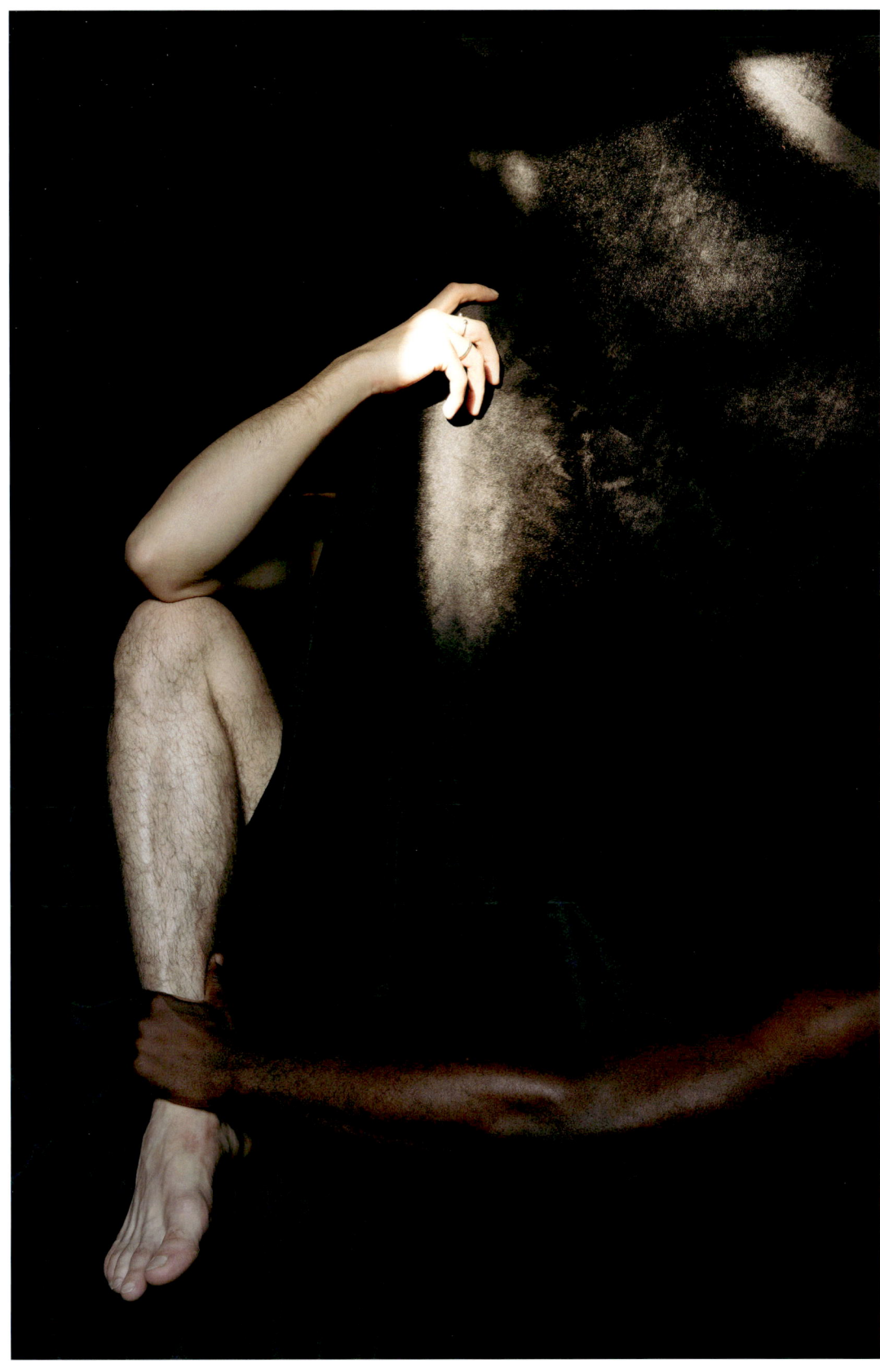

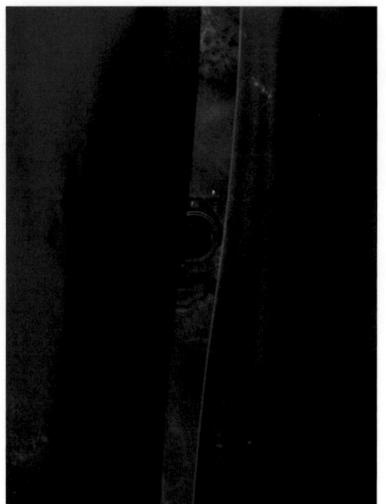 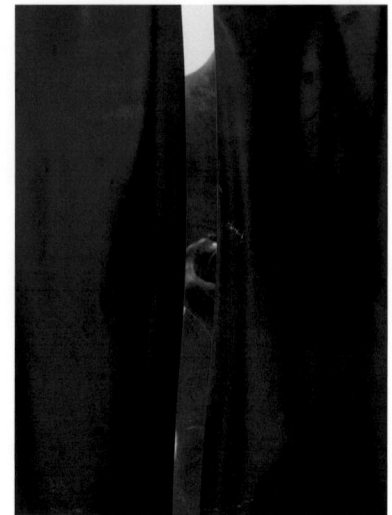

Exposure (_2100879), 2017   *Exposure (_2100889)*, 2017

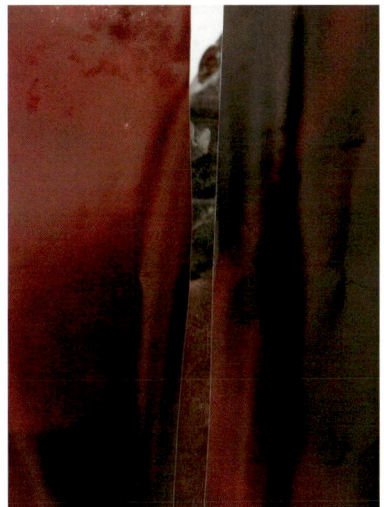 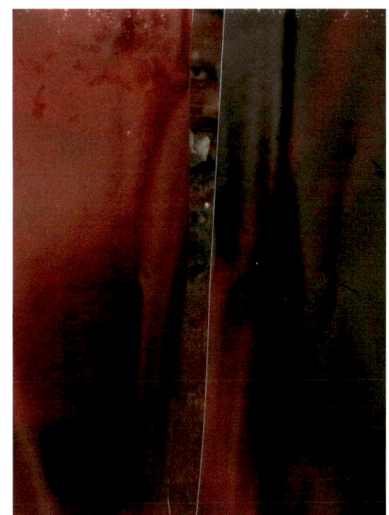 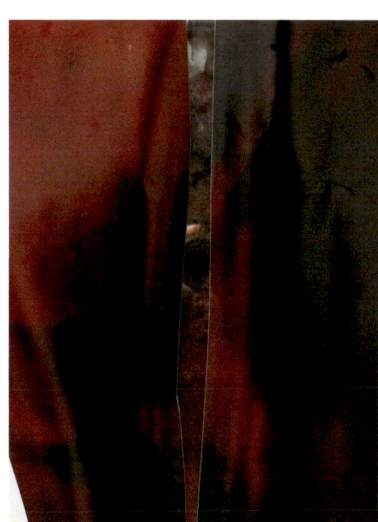

Exposure (_2100999), 2017   *Exposure (_2110004)*, 2017   *Exposure (_2110008)*, 2017

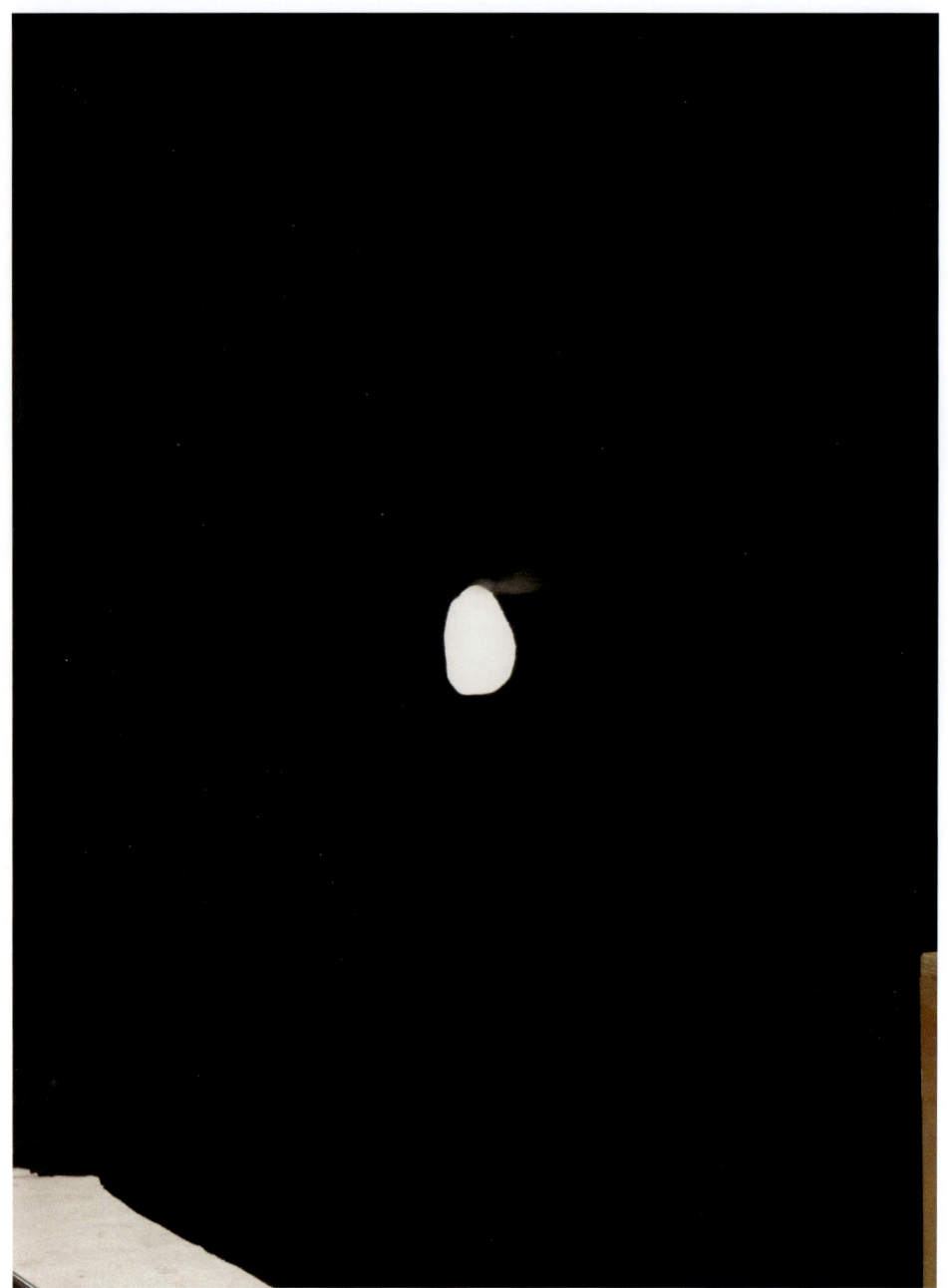

Aperture (_2140020), 2018

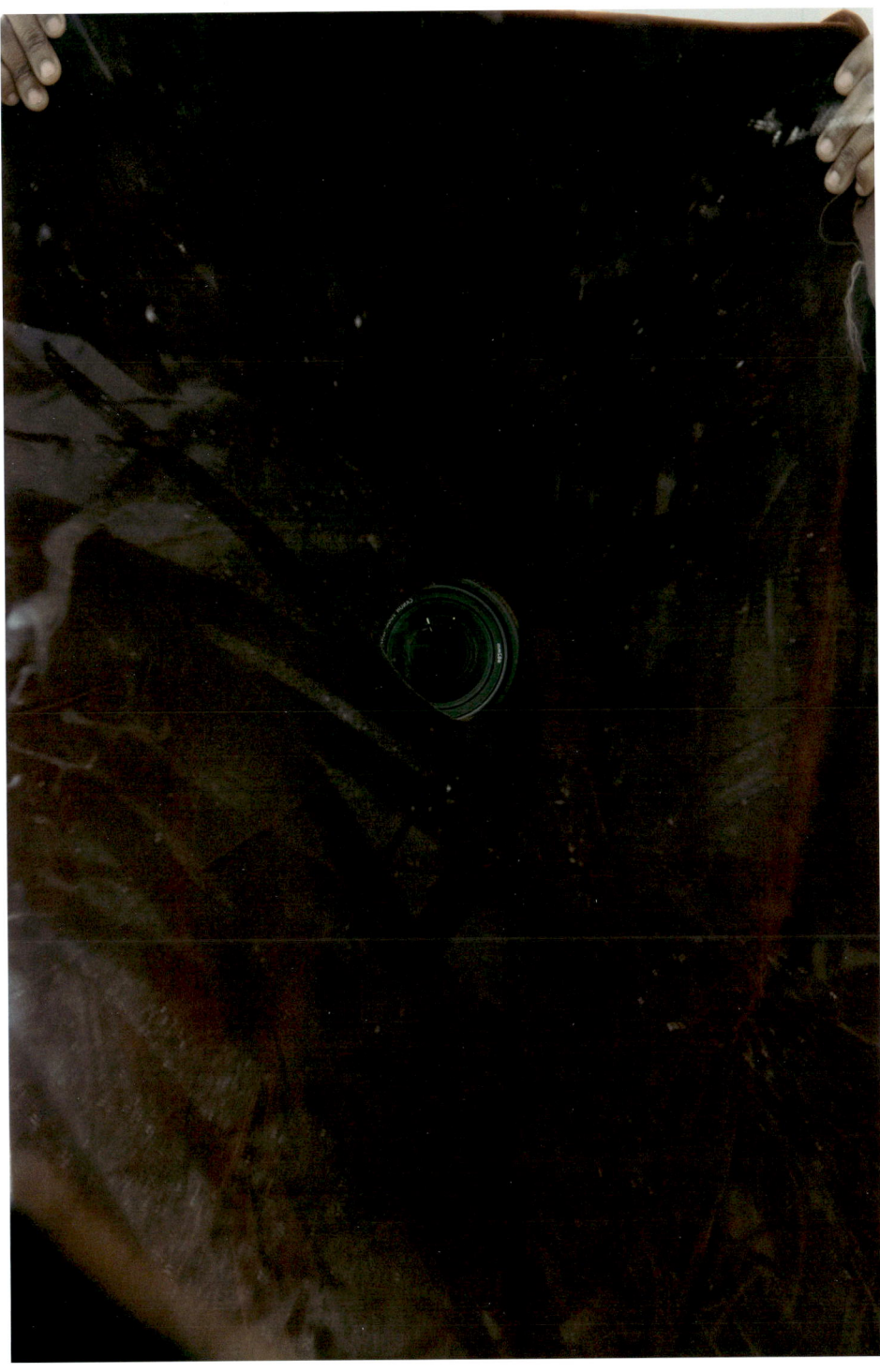

Orifice (0X5A6982), 2018

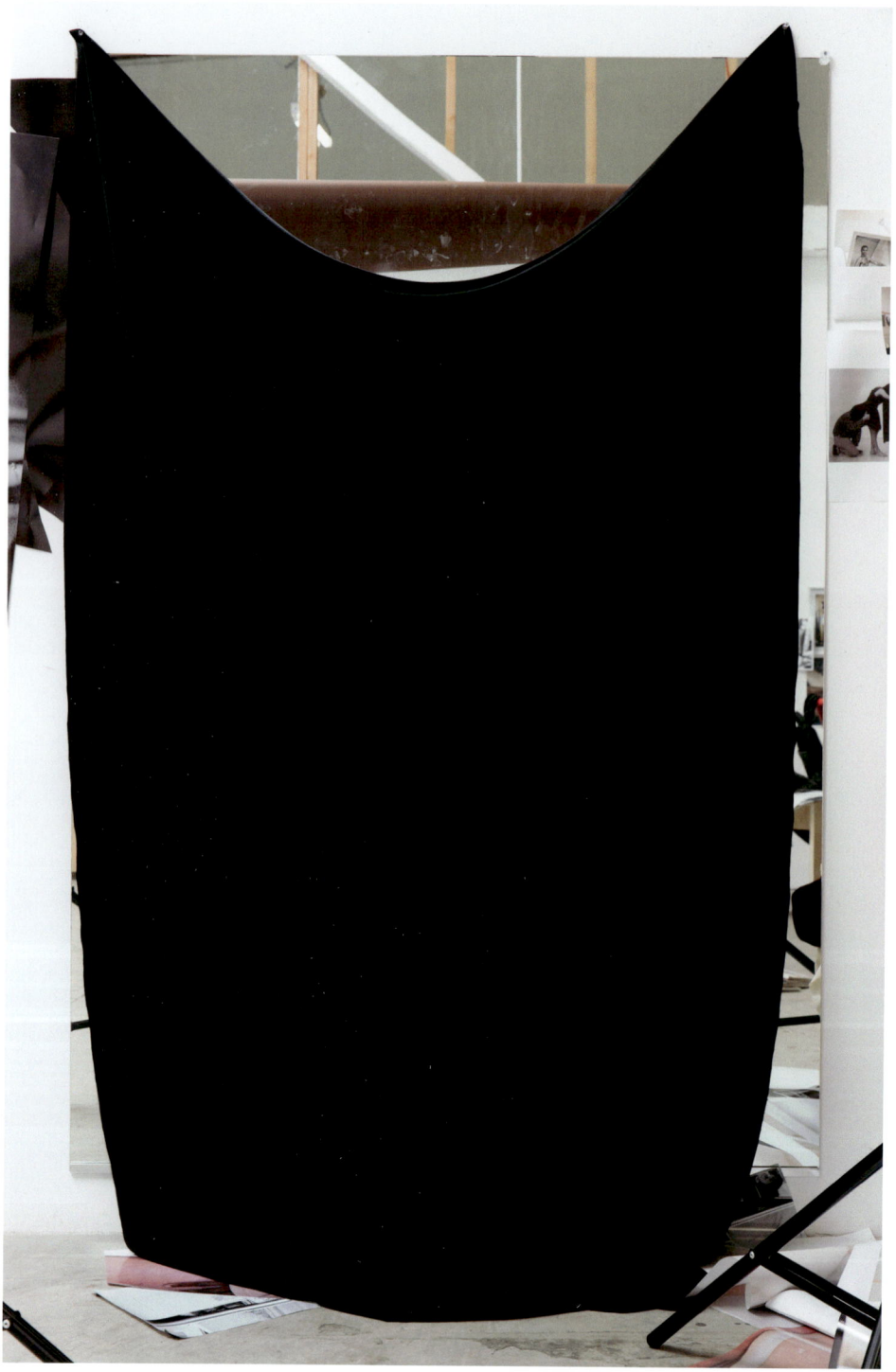

A Ground (0X5A1495), 2018

Exhibition Checklist

The exhibition checklist appears in order of the plates

Early Portraits

Rafi, 2005
C-print
9 3/5 × 7 1/2 in.
20 1/2 × 18 1/2 in. framed
Courtesy the artist and Vielmetter Los Angeles

Self Portrait Holding Joshua's Hand, 2006
C-print
14 × 11 in.
25 × 22 in. framed
Courtesy the artist and Vielmetter Los Angeles

Tyler, 2008
C-print
9 3/5 × 7 1/2 in.
20 1/2 × 18 1/2 in. framed
Courtesy the artist and Vielmetter Los Angeles

Pericles, 2008
C-print
9 3/5 × 7 1/2 in.
21 × 19 in. framed
Courtesy the artist and Vielmetter Los Angeles

Devin, 2008
C-print
9 3/5 × 7 1/2 in.
20 1/2 × 18 1/2 in. framed
Courtesy the artist and Vielmetter Los Angeles

Marques (Adriano, Marques, Henning), 2008
C-print
9 × 7 in.
20 1/2 × 18 1/2 in. framed
Courtesy the artist and Vielmetter Los Angeles

Ben, 2009
C-print
9 3/5 × 7 1/2 in.
20 1/2 × 18 1/2 in. framed
Courtesy the artist and Vielmetter Los Angeles

STUDIO WORK, 2010–11

STUDIO WORK, 2010–11
Books, magazines, papers, laser prints on paper,
digital C-prints (8 × 10, 4 × 6, and various sizes),
medium-format instant photographs, pushpins,
Post-it notes, bookmarks, bricks, store-bought
frames, dried orange peels, bread, glass, manila
envelopes, unsolicited letter, clips, shipping
boxes, fabric, bubble wrap, shipping crate
Crate size: 28 × 25 1/2 × 28 1/4 in.
Courtesy the artist and Vielmetter Los Angeles

Darren, September 8, 2011
Archival pigment print
24 × 18 in.
31 × 25 in. framed
Courtesy the artist and DOCUMENT, Chicago

Some Recent Pictures, 2013–14

Studio, March 12, 2014
Archival pigment print
24 × 18 in.
31 × 25 in. framed
Courtesy the artist and DOCUMENT, Chicago

Studio, March 2 (part 1), 2014
Archival pigment print
24 × 18 in.
31 × 25 in. framed
Courtesy the artist and DOCUMENT, Chicago

Studio, March 2 (part 2), 2014
Archival pigment print
24 × 18 in.
31 × 25 in. framed
Courtesy the artist and DOCUMENT, Chicago

Desktop, April 2, 2014
Archival pigment print
24 × 18 in.
30 × 24 in. framed
Courtesy the artist and DOCUMENT, Chicago
*Included in exhibition at Blaffer Art Museum,
University of Houston

Robert, March 24, 2014
Archival pigment print
48 × 36 in.
49 × 37 in. framed
Courtesy the artist and DOCUMENT, Chicago

Kitchen, Brooklyn, March 3, 2013–15
Archival pigment print
32 × 24 in.
33 × 25 in. framed
Courtesy the artist and DOCUMENT, Chicago

Studies

Study for T.H. with Two Figures (2005), 2015
Archival pigment print
48 × 34 in.
49 × 40½ in. framed
Courtesy the artist and DOCUMENT, Chicago

Five Figures (3002), 2016
Archival pigment print
80 × 60 in.
81 × 61 in. framed
Courtesy the artist and Vielmetter Los Angeles

Study for friendship, D.C.S. and F.C. (2106), 2015
Archival pigment print
48 × 34 in.
49 × 38 in. framed
Courtesy the artist and DOCUMENT, Chicago

Mirror Study for Grace (0X5A2066), 2017
Archival pigment print
24 × 16 in.
24¾ × 16¾ in. framed
Courtesy the artist and team (gallery, inc.)

Studio (0X5A0173), 2017
Archival pigment print
75 × 50 in.
76½ × 51½ in. framed
Courtesy the artist and team (gallery, inc.)
*Included in exhibition at Blaffer Art Museum,
University of Houston

Studio Wall (_1000021), 2018
Archival pigment print
45 × 34 in.
46¼ × 35¼ in. framed
Courtesy the artist and team (gallery, inc.)

Studio (_2150762), 2017
Archival pigment print
24 × 18 in.
25 × 19 in. framed
Courtesy the artist and team (gallery, inc.)

Mirror Studies

A Ground (File0083), 2015
Archival pigment print
13 × 10 in.
24½ × 20½ in. framed
Courtesy the artist and DOCUMENT, Chicago

Study (_R2A9181), 2015
Archival pigment print
13 × 9 in.
24½ × 20½ in. framed
Courtesy the artist and DOCUMENT, Chicago

Figure Ground Study (_2000769), 2017
Archival pigment print
13 × 10 in.
25 × 21½ in. framed
Collection of the artist

Mirror Study (_Q5A2097), 2016
Archival pigment print
13 × 9 in.
24¾ × 20¾ in. framed
Collection of Sibylle Friche and Daniel Quiles,
Chicago

Mirror Study (4R2A0857), 2016
Archival pigment print
51 × 34 in.
52 × 35 in. framed
Collection of Joshua Friedman, Los Angeles

Mirror Study for Joe (_2010980), 2017
Archival pigment print
45 × 34 in.
46 × 34¾ in. framed
Private collection, Chicago

Figure (_2010037), 2017
Archival pigment print
32 × 24 in.
32¾ × 24¾ in. framed
Collection of Mark McDonald and Dwayne
Resnick, New York
*Exhibition at Blaffer Art Museum, University of
Houston, included an edition from the collection
of Lina Hargrett and Carlos Lago, Miami

Mirror Study (0X5A1317), 2017
Archival pigment print
51 × 34 in.
52½ × 35 in. framed
Collection of Hedy Fischer and Randy Shull,
Asheville, NC

Mirror Study (0X5A7394), 2018
Archival pigment print
51 × 34 in.
52 × 35 in. framed
Collection of Columbus Museum of Art, Ohio:
Museum purchase with funds provided by the
Contemporaries

Mirror Study (0X5A7421), 2018
Archival pigment print
51 × 34 in.
52 × 35 in. framed
Courtesy the artist and team (gallery, inc.)

A Portrait (0X5A6109), 2017
Archival pigment print
75 × 50 in.
76½ × 51½ in. framed
Courtesy the artist and team (gallery, inc.)
*Included in exhibition at Blaffer Art Museum,
University of Houston

Dark Room

Model Study (0X5A3973), 2017
Archival pigment print
75 × 50 in.
76½ × 51½ in. framed
Courtesy the artist and team (gallery, inc.)
*Included in exhibition at Blaffer Art Museum,
University of Houston

A Portrait (0X5A8325), 2018
Archival pigment print
51 × 34 in.
52¼ × 35¼ in. framed
Courtesy the artist and team (gallery, inc.)
*Included in exhibition at Blaffer Art Museum,
University of Houston

Darkroom Mirror Study (_1990750), 2016
Archival pigment print
13 × 10 in.
24½ × 20½ in. framed
Courtesy the artist and DOCUMENT, Chicago

Darkroom Mirror Study (0X5A1531), 2017
Archival pigment print
51 × 34 in.
52 × 35 in. framed
Collection of Hedy Fischer and Randy Shull,
Asheville, NC

Darkroom Mirror Study (0X5A1812), 2017
Archival pigment print
51 × 34 in.
52 × 35 in. framed
Courtesy the artist and team (gallery, inc.)

Darkroom Mirror (_2070386), 2017
Archival pigment print
32 × 24 in.
32½ × 24½ in. framed
Collection of the artist

Darkroom Mirror (_2060999), 2017
Archival pigment print
13 × 10 in.
24½ × 20¾ in. framed
Collection of the artist

Dark Room (0X5A2919), 2017
Archival pigment print
51 × 34 in.
52 × 35 in. framed
Courtesy the artist and DOCUMENT, Chicago

Exposure (_2100879), 2017
Archival pigment print
32 × 24 in.
32¾ × 24¾ in. framed
Courtesy the artist and DOCUMENT, Chicago

Exposure (_2100889), 2017
Archival pigment print
32 × 24 in.
32¾ × 24¾ in. framed
Courtesy the artist and DOCUMENT, Chicago

Exposure (_2100999), 2017
Archival pigment print
32 × 24 in.
32¾ × 24¾ in. framed
Courtesy the artist and DOCUMENT, Chicago

Exposure (_2110004), 2017
Archival pigment print
32 × 24 in.
32¾ × 24¾ in. framed
Courtesy the artist and DOCUMENT, Chicago

Exposure (_2110008), 2017
Archival pigment print
32 × 24 in.
32¾ × 24¾ in. framed
Courtesy the artist and DOCUMENT, Chicago

Aperture (_2140020), 2018
Archival pigment print
32 × 24 in.
33¼ × 25¼ in. framed
Courtesy the artist and team (gallery, inc.)

Orifice (0X5A6982), 2018
Archival pigment print
31⅝ × 23⅝ in.
33¼ × 25¼ in. framed
Courtesy the artist and team (gallery, inc.)

A Ground (0X5A1495), 2018
Archival pigment print
51 × 34 in.
52 × 35 in. framed
Courtesy the artist and DOCUMENT, Chicago

Not included in plates section

Mirror Study for Grace (0X5A2020), 2017
Archival pigment print
24 × 16 in.
25 × 16¾ in. framed
Private collection, New York

Contributor Biographies

Compiled by Misa Jeffereis, Assistant Curator

Paul Mpagi Sepuya (born in San Bernadino, California, 1982) is a Los Angeles–based artist working in photography. His work is in the collections of The Museum of Modern Art (MoMA), Whitney Museum of American Art, Guggenheim Museum, the Studio Museum in Harlem, and MOCA Los Angeles, among others. Sepuya's most recent gallery exhibition, *The Conditions* at team (gallery, inc.), New York (2019), was reviewed in *The New Yorker*, *The New York Times*, and *Art in America*, and he was featured on the cover of *Artforum*'s March 2019 issue. A survey of work from 2005 to 2018 premiered at the Contemporary Art Museum St. Louis in 2019, and Sepuya was included in the 2019 Whitney Biennial and in exhibitions at the Guggenheim Museum and the Getty Museum. Recent exhibitions include *Being: New Photography 2018* at MoMA and *Double Enclosure* at Fotomuseum Amsterdam (2018), Sepuya's first museum exhibition in Europe. He is acting associate professor in media arts at the University of California, San Diego.

Wassan Al-Khudhairi is chief curator at the Contemporary Art Museum St. Louis, where she has organized *Paul Mpagi Sepuya*; *Lawrence Abu Hamdan: Earwitness Theatre*; *Guan Xiao: Fiction Archive Project*; *Hayv Kahraman: Acts of Reparation*; *Trenton Doyle Hancock: The Re-Evolving Door to the Moundverse*; and *SUPERFLEX: European Union Mayotte*. Prior to her position at CAM, Al-Khudhairi was the Hugh Kaul Curator of Modern and Contemporary Art at the Birmingham Museum of Art, Alabama, where she organized the first large-scale exhibition of the museum's contemporary collection, *Third Space / shifting conversations about contemporary art*. Al-Khudhairi was a curator for the 6th Asian Art Biennial in Taiwan in 2017 and co-artistic director for the 9th Gwangju Biennial in South Korea in 2012. As the founding director of Mathaf: Arab Museum of Modern Art in Qatar, Al-Khudhairi oversaw the opening of the museum in 2010, co-curated *Sajjil: A Century of Modern Art*, and curated *Cai Guo-Qiang: Saraab*.

Malik Gaines is an artist and writer based in New York. He is the author of *Black Performance on the Outskirts of the Left: A History of the Impossible* (2017), which traces a transnational circulation of political ideas through performances of the 1960s and beyond, and was nominated for a Lambda Literary Award. Since 2000, Gaines has performed and exhibited extensively with the group My Barbarian, whose work has been included in the Whitney Biennial, Performa Biennial, Montreal Biennial, and Baltic Triennial, among others. Gaines is associate professor of performance studies at New York University's Tisch School of the Arts.

Lucy Gallun is associate curator in the Department of Photography at The Museum of Modern Art in New York. She has curated and co-curated multiple exhibitions at MoMA, including *Being: New Photography 2018*, which featured multiple works by Paul Mpagi Sepuya; *Projects 108: Gauri Gill* at MoMA PS1; *Unfinished Conversations: New Work from the Collection*; *Soldier, Spectre, Shaman: The Figure and the Second World War*; and many others. Gallun is also co-editor of a three-volume history, *Photography at MoMA*. Prior to joining MoMA, Gallun was the Whitney-Lauder Curatorial Fellow at the Institute of Contemporary Art in Philadelphia, and she was a Helena Rubinstein Curatorial Fellow at the Whitney Museum Independent Study Program.

Ariel Goldberg is a writer based in Queens, New York. Their publications include *The Estrangement Principle* (2016) and *The Photographer* (2015). From 2014 to 2017 they organized readings at The Poetry Project. Goldberg's art criticism has appeared in *e-flux*, *Artforum*, *Afterimage*, and *Art in America*. They have taught art writing at Pratt Institute, The New School, and Columbia University. Goldberg was the 2018–19 Zuckerman Fellow, Curator of Community Engagement at the Jewish History Museum in Tucson.

Evan Moffitt is a writer, editor, and critic based in New York. His writing appears regularly in *frieze*, where he is associate editor. His work has been featured in various publications, including *Aperture*, *Apollo*, *Art in America*, *BOMB*, *Brooklyn Rail*, *Flash Art*, *PARIS LA*, *PIN-UP*, *Transition Magazine*, and the *White Review*; as well as the *Los Angeles Review of Books*, where he served as assistant editor from 2014 to 2015, and *Contemporary Art Review Los Angeles*, where he served as associate editor. He has contributed to catalogs on artists, including Brendan Fernandes, Barbara Wagner, and Benjamin de Burca, and spoken at numerous institutions, such as Centre Pompidou, Pinacoteca do Estado de São Paulo, Hammer Museum, International Center of Photography, and New York University.

Grace Wales Bonner is creative director and founder of Wales Bonner, a menswear brand based in London. Informed by broad research encompassing critical theory, musical composition, literature, and history, Wales Bonner embraces a multiplicity of perspectives, proposing a distinct notion of luxury, via a hybrid of European and Afro-Atlantic approaches. Since graduating from Central Saint Martins in 2014, Wales Bonner has received accolades, including Emerging Menswear Designer at the British Fashion Awards 2015, the 2016 LVMH Prize, and the BFC/Vogue Fashion Fund. In 2019, Wales Bonner presented the exhibition *A Time for New Dreams* at London's Serpentine Galleries.

Published on the occasion of the exhibition
Paul Mpagi Sepuya
Contemporary Art Museum St. Louis
May 17–August 18, 2019
Blaffer Art Museum, University of Houston
October 19, 2019–March 14, 2020

Organized by Wassan Al-Khudhairi, chief curator, with Misa Jeffereis, assistant curator

The exhibition and catalog are generously supported by the Robert Mapplethorpe Foundation; DOCUMENT, Chicago; team (gallery, inc.); Vielmetter Los Angeles; Hedy Fischer and Randy Shull; Nancy and Fred Poses; Hunt R. Tackbary; Heiji and Brian Black; and Thomas Lavin.

Contemporary Art Museum St. Louis

3750 Washington Boulevard
St. Louis, MO 63108
camstl.org

Published in association with

aperture

Aperture Foundation
548 West 28th Street, 4th floor
New York, NY 10001
aperture.org

Aperture staff for this book:
Creative Director: Lesley A. Martin
Associate Editor: Samantha Marlow
Publishing Manager: Taia Kwinter
Senior Text Editor: Susan Ciccotti
Proofreader: Elena Goukassian
Work Scholar: Jamie Bernstein

Additional support for this catalog is provided by Michael Hoeh

To order Aperture books or inquire about gift or group orders, contact:
+1 212.946.7154
orders@aperture.org

For information about Aperture trade distribution worldwide, visit:
aperture.org/distribution

Aperture, a not-for-profit foundation, connects the photo community and its audiences with the most inspiring work, the sharpest ideas, and with each other—in print, in person, and online.

Produced by Lucia | Marquand, Seattle
luciamarquand.com
Designed by Thomas Eykemans
Edited by Misa Jeffereis and Eddie Silva
Typeset by Tina Henderson
Proofread by Ivy Gilley
Printed in China by Artron Art Group
Photography by Dusty Kessler: pages 2, 4, 7, 9

Pages 2, 4, 7, 9: *Paul Mpagi Sepuya*, installation view, Contemporary Art Museum St. Louis, May 17–August 18, 2019. Photo: Dusty Kessler.

First edition, 2020
10 9 8 7 6 5 4 3 2

Library of Congress Control Number:
2019917930
ISBN 978-1-59711-480-6